Better Homes and Gardens®

Basement

PLANNER

Better Homes and Gardens® Books
Des Moines, Iowa

Better Homes and Gardens® Books
An imprint of Meredith® Books

Name of Book
Editor: Brian Kramer
Project Editor: Jan Soults Walker
Contributing Editors: Cathy Kramer, Elaine Markoutsas, Bill Nolan
Senior Associate Design Director: Mick Schnepf
Designer: David Jordan
Copy Chief: Terri Fredrickson
Copy and Production Editor: Victoria Forlini
Editorial Operations Manager: Karen Schirm
Managers, Book Production: Pam Kvitne, Marjorie J. Schenkelberg, Rick von Holdt
Contributing Copy Editor: Steve Hallam
Contributing Proofreaders: Judy Friedman, David Krause, Sue Fetters
Contributing Photographers: Guy Hurka, Geoff Johnson
Contributing Illustrator: Tom Stocki
Indexer: Beverley A. Nightenhelser
Electronic Production Coordinator: Paula Forest
Editorial and Design Assistants: Kaye Chabot, Karen McFadden, Mary Lee Gavin

Meredith® Books
Editor in Chief: Linda Raglan Cunningham
Design Director: Matt Strelecki
Executive Editor, Home Decorating and Design: Denise L. Caringer

Publisher: James D. Blume
Executive Director, Marketing: Jeffrey Myers
Executive Director, New Business Development: Todd M. Davis
Executive Director, Sales: Ken Zagor
Director, Operations: George A. Susral
Director, Production: Douglas M. Johnston
Business Director: Jim Leonard

Vice President and General Manager: Douglas J. Guendel

Better Homes and Gardens® Magazine
Editor in Chief: Karol DeWulf Nickell

Meredith Publishing Group
President, Publishing Group: Stephen M. Lacy
Vice President-Publishing Director: Bob Mate

Meredith Corporation
Chairman and Chief Executive Officer: William T. Kerr

In Memoriam: E. T. Meredith III (1933–2003)

All of us at Better Homes and Gardens® Books are dedicated to providing you with information and ideas to enhance your home. We welcome your comments and suggestions. Write to us at: Better Homes and Gardens Books, Home Decorating and Design Editorial Department, 1716 Locust St., Des Moines, IA 50309-3023.

If you would like to purchase any of our home decorating and design, cooking, crafts, gardening, or home improvement books, check wherever quality books are sold. Or visit us at: bhgbooks.com

Cover Photograph: Geoff Johnson, Malone & Company Photography

Contents

Dare to Dream

Planning comfortable living spaces in the basement begins with envisioning all it can become.

Think of it as sunken treasure. This very moment you may be sitting directly above an untapped gold mine of square footage. If your home features an unfinished, unappreciated basement, then you already own the extra space you're searching for. Because exterior walls, the floor, and the ceiling are already in place, finishing a basement to gain inviting and functional rooms can be an affordable alternative to building an addition.

Basements offer other potential benefits, such as privacy, buffers against noise, and pleasantly cool temperatures during hot weather. In winter climates, basement rooms can easily be designed for warmth. If moisture, lack of light, and poor access are issues, you're about to discover remedies for each of these common basement problems. You'll find the planning process manageable as you learn to evaluate, shape, appoint, decorate, and budget for your basement to gain beauty and function.

First, take a few minutes to imagine the exciting living spaces you could carve from this unclaimed treasure.

Opposite: When this walkout ranch expanded, the basement was dug a little deeper to include plenty of space on the lower level for family gatherings. The new room triples the original size of the old recreation area to make way for a bar, a pool table, and a spacious, comfortable conversation area. To create extra headroom, part of the new area steps down about a foot. An alcove on one wall houses a 51-inch television screen that's topped with built-in shelves and cabinets for display and storage.

Ready to make the list of best cellars? Plot your basement layout with a few stylish twists on tradition, such as this bar that angles across the space rather than running parallel to the wall.

A Warm Invitation

Gone are the days of dropped acoustic ceilings in unattractive patterns, faux-wood paneling, and indoor/outdoor carpeting. Today's eye-pleasing materials, finishes, and furnishings that beautify upper-level living spaces easily transition into the basement. Warm woods, sunny colors, comfortable seating, and entertainment amenities assure that guests won't feel confined in the basement, but will revel in the inviting surroundings. As you consider options for your unfinished basement, think about how you would most like to relax or entertain, then make your decisions accordingly. To accommodate either a quiet evening with your family or a crowd of friends for a party, for example, don't rely on walls to form activity areas for drinks, dinner, conversation, or recreation. To define areas for specific functions, vary the levels of your floor and ceiling, and strategically locate lighting.

Interior windows visually connect this home office to the recreation area of the basement, allowing the homeowners to work while still keeping tabs on children playing in the adjacent room. The interior window also does a great job of admitting additional light yet buffering noise.

Just For Kids

Children are thrilled by any space where they can indulge their imaginations. That includes wide-open spaces for spreading out and setting up art tables, racetracks, and theaters, or for a secret nook—such as one tucked beneath basement stairs—where they can burrow and dream. Basements are ideal places for playrooms because messes stay out of main living areas and boisterous games and giggles won't interrupt activities upstairs. Whatever type of space your project involves, think ahead to when the children are grown. If you're finishing unfinished space now, spare yourself greater expense by installing wiring, plumbing, or soundproofing you may want later.

Because this part of the basement lacks natural light, it is a sensible choice for a theater-type playroom with a raised stage at one end. An exercise room next to the stage doubles as a dressing room and a stage entrance.

Left: Candy-colored wall paint and black-and-white sheet vinyl flooring make this block wall/cement slab play space cheerful and fun. Another standout feature is the ceiling treatment: Wave after wave of polka-dot fabric stapled to floor joists creates a party-tent effect and conceals pipes.

Below: Decorated canvas backdrops open to reveal a surprise at the back of the stage—a built-in niche for a large-screen television. Lounge chairs provide movable seating for the theater, and track lights gracefully step in as set lighting.

A Place For Parties

If you're looking for a place to have parties for adults or teens, have fun with a theme that inspires good times. Because basements are separate from main living areas, don't be afraid to explore your adventurous side when decorating. They're great spaces for indulging a dream, experimenting with bold color, or displaying a large collection. To keep noise out of other parts of the house, install insulation in the ceiling and walls of your basement before applying drywall or paneling. Be sure to plan a location for stereo equipment and wiring for speakers throughout the room. Choose easy-to-clean materials that withstand spills and heavy traffic.

Opposite and below: Black-and-white adhesive vinyl tiles give a classic look to this imaginative reproduction of a 1950s diner, complete with cool blue-vinyl booths and a soda fountain. For more visual excitement, a false wall incorporates a band of glass blocks that can be illuminated from behind. The dropped soffit adds architectural interest and cleverly disguises ducts, wires, and pipes.

This basement media room is finished with knotty white-pine siding for a comfortable lodge look. Distressed leather furnishings and hollowed-out pine logs epitomize the ambience as they conceal structural steel posts. Speakers hide under the TV screen, tucked behind black grille cloth and a crating lumber frame. Commercial-grade carpeting and a rubber pad cover the concrete slab. Unlike foam, rubber does not deteriorate in humid conditions.

Private Screening

You don't need to drive across town for a movie. Bring it home by finishing your basement to include

a private media room with a big-screen television, surround sound system, and sink-in seating. A

media room takes advantage of a basement's natural assets: darkness, separation from household

activity, and shape. Most basements are rectangular—the shape audio-video experts recommend

for rich, realistic sound. Experts also suggest placing rugs or carpet over hard floors. Hard surfaces

increase sound distortion; fabrics reduce it. While you'll find it helpful to understand the basics of

planning a home theater, consulting an installation professional can help you achieve the optimum

In the center of the library wall, doors open to reveal a television, VCR, CD/DVD player, and sound system. The opened doors recess into the storage unit while the equipment is in use. Shelves in lower cabinets roll out (inset) so CDs, DVDs, and videos are more accessible.

listening and viewing environment. (For more information on planning a home theater, turn to page 70.) While you're at it, pencil a mini-bar into your plans and don't forget to include a microwave oven for making popcorn.

Here's To Health

Wedging a fitness routine into your schedule is easy when you have a gym set up at home. Sneak in a yoga session before the kids wake up or do a round of weights while dinner simmers. Your gym doesn't need to rival the local health club; just make it functional, comfortable, and inviting.

Durable vinyl flooring and an energizing color scheme create an attractive space for exercise routines. A small bump-out topped with a greenhouse window draws plenty of light into this basement level area.

Select tough flooring such as vinyl, cork, or if carpet is appropriate, a tightly woven style that cushions your step without cramping your routine. Create the illusion of a larger space with a floor-to-ceiling mirror, which also helps you observe your exercising form and technique. Be sure to install enough outlets to accommodate a music system and a television as well as a VCR or DVD player.

To expand on a fitness theme, consider including a sauna in your basement plans. (See page 85 for more information on saunas.)

You don't have to dedicate an entire room to exercise if you don't have the space. This bath squeezes in a treadmill just beyond a partial wall. You're more likely to regularly use a treadmill where there is a pleasant window view or a television to watch as you pick up the pace.

Including a mirror in your exercise room allows you to check for proper positioning during a movement. It also makes the lower-level space appear brighter, larger, and more inviting.

Hospitality Suites

Below right: A mini-kitchen can be as much a convenience for overnight guests as it is for parties. In one small slice of space, this area features storage, a countertop, an undercounter refrigerator, and a bar sink. The translucent panel behind the mini-kitchen admits sunlight into the home office (shown on page 111).

Below: Close the pocket door, and the bathroom teams up with the adjacent office to serve as a welcoming, private guest suite.

Whether you need a private suite for a live-in nanny or welcoming accommodations for overnight guests, the basement can be the ideal location for a guest bedroom, bathroom, and mini-kitchen. The combination of good lighting, inviting materials, and comfortable temperatures will make anyone feel at home. Basements tend to stay cool in summer, so air-conditioning may not be needed; however, you may want an additional heat source to keep a bedroom and bathroom cozy. In-floor radiant heating (see page 53 for more information) is a wonderful solution for keeping toes toasty during cold days.

Remember that sleeping rooms in the basement require at least one window as an emergency exit. (For more on adding windows to the lower level, see page 48.)

Honey-stained hardwood flooring, plenty of light, and a silk ficus tree give this basement bedroom a welcoming look while dark furnishings add richness. The dominant feature of this room's success is fluorescent tubes mounted behind the shuttered wall that bathe the room in soft, natural-looking light. The shutters also introduce textural interest and provide a backdrop from which to hang artwork.

An eye for detail during the planning stage can allow you to fit in special features—even in a modest-size space. A small nook behind the basement stairs is perfect for tucking in this bar area that features granite countertops, a small refrigerator, a built-in wine rack, and storage for glassware.

Small Space Tactics

Even small basements can yield multiple uses when you downsize furnishings, choose pieces that

offer more than one function, and include storage and work surfaces to accommodate other activ-

ities and pastimes. Look for ottomans and benches with interior storage, for example. A living area

or home office by day can become a bedroom at night with the addition of a Murphy bed that folds down out of the wall or a daybed that doubles as a sofa and a bed. Tall cabinets, such as armoires, take advantage of vertical space for storage. Or plan an entire wall of built-in cabinetry that includes open shelves and a fold-down table. Design inside-the-wall storage to make room for other activities such as sewing, playing games, or doing homework.

Stylish overstuffed furnishings make a basement feel cozy. A comfy hide-a-bed, such as this one, can allow a small lower-level family room to double as a guest room for overnight visitors.

Creative Corner

Fitted with French doors and a tiled floor, this walkout basement is an elegant, light-filled painter's studio. Open the windows and pull up a table, and the space quickly converts to an alfresco dining area.

Away from the core of household activity, basements make wonderful locations for a home office, a homework/computer room, or a specially equipped space for exploring creative interests. You'll marvel at the inspiration and productivity that come from having a place dedicated to your work or your hobbies, a place where all your supplies, tools, and materials are close at hand. To organize supplies, consider a wall of modular shelves, drawers, and cabinets. You can find your supplies at a glance in see-through bins. Include a generous-size worktable and comfortable stools, and make sure your work area is well-lit. (For more on lighting your basement, see page 68. Additional information on planning a home office is on page 74.)

Left: A chalkboard wall (it's actually chalkboard paint), a run of built-in desks, and bin-style hardware create an inviting learning center. As the family's needs change, shelves can be cleared to make way for books, collectibles, or home office materials.

Below: By placing an exhaust fan in the window and hooking saws and other tools to dust-collection systems, this home shop stays extra clean. The wall cabinets are mounted over the pegboard wall on support strips, so the cabinets can be lifted off and moved to new locations as shop needs change.

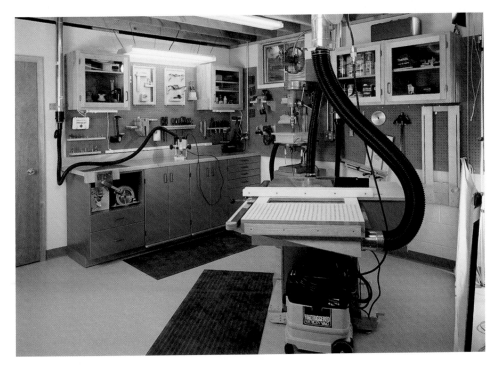

For Connoisseurs

Opposite: Floor-to-ceiling racks in this walk-in wine room allow storage of a large number of bottles in a relatively small space. The arched window isn't just attractive; it opens to access a ledge where a bartender can serve drinks and wine during parties.
Far right: A glass door on this walk-in wine cooler allows an extensive collection of wine to always remain on display.
Right: Inside, uniquely designed zigzag racks cleverly display the collection.

The inherently cool climate of the basement makes it a natural place to store wines. The best wine cellars duplicate natural conditions found in underground caves in France and Italy where winemakers have been storing wine for hundreds of years. To maintain the suggested 57-degree temperature, however, you'll probably need a cooling system and insulation in the walls and ceiling, as well as a polyethylene vapor barrier. Of course, if you don't want to dedicate an entire room to wine storage, you can finish a closet-size space or custom fit a manufactured wine cooler. (For more information on creating a wine cellar or closet, turn to page 86.)

Simplify Chores

Yellow paint and white vintage-style shelves bring sunny appeal to this once-dark basement laundry room in an early 1900s house. When not in use, the ironing board conveniently slides into a drawer opening.

Routine chores become less tiresome when you're organized, and finishing the basement presents an opportunity to assess your needs for a well-equipped laundry room. If you're short on space, consider a stacked washer and dryer, which will fit into a closet-size area. A fold-down ironing board is another space-saver. For added convenience, include a laundry chute. A countertop makes folding clothes easy on the spot, and a rod or rack near the dryer and ironing board help you hang clothing fresh from the dryer. (For more on planning a laundry center, turn to page 82.)

Wire baskets store dirty laundry and supplies; a long countertop is just right for folding. The small undercounter refrigerator keeps snacks and beverages close at hand.

Adjacent to the washing/ironing area is a built-in desk that's topped with the same blue laminate as the countertops. Bookkeeping, letter writing, and general household organizational tasks can be done here while waiting for the next spin cycle. A faux window above the desk makes the windowless room feel open and interesting.

Evaluate Your Basement

Before you can make your dreams come true, take the first steps to claiming your basement as living space: Assess the condition of your below-grade space and correct any potential problems.

Opposite: **Striking special features such as the paneling, furnishings, and a rug in this basement are worth the investment. Before adding such lovely features, make sure your basement is in the best shape it can be, is moisture-free, and conforms to codes.**

Could your current basement be used as a set for a horror flick on *Midnight Creature Feature Theater*—complete with dim lighting, damp air, cracked walls, and ice-cold floors? You just can't spend quality time in that kind of environment. Prepare to make the switch from creepy to cozy as you learn in this chapter how to spot, identify the cause of, and clear up moisture problems (one of the most common basement ills). Along the way you'll get sound advice on how to repair walls and floors, assess window and stair access needs, and investigate other code requirements. Resolving all these issues before you finish below-grade space with quality materials protects your investment and yields additional living space that's as light, inviting, dry, and comfortable as any of your upper-level rooms.

Eliminate Moisture

Tape squares of aluminum foil to different spots on the basement floor and walls, using duct tape to secure the edges. Leave the foil in place for several days. Droplets collecting on the underside of the foil indicate water seeping in from outside; droplets atop the foil point to condensation.

Water in a basement can be caused by something as simple as clogged downspouts to a more complicated scenario, such as a rising water table. Fortunately, most cures for wet basements aren't costly. Here's a look at the possible problems and solutions.

Condensation or leaks?

When warm air comes in contact with cool basement walls and floors as well as plumbing pipes, condensation can occur. If water problems seem to clear up in summer when windows and doors are closed and the air-conditioner is running, condensation could be the culprit. Water collecting on the floor or dampness on walls or pipes isn't always condensation, however, but could be signs of leaks or seepage. To determine the source of the water, perform the simple test *left*.

Excess humidity—which can be elevated by such internal sources as a basement shower, washing machine, or unvented dryer—can lead to damp walls, dripping pipes, and mildewed surfaces. To alleviate this condensation, improve ventilation in the basement by installing ventilating fans or opening windows during mild weather. You can also seal interior walls and install a dehumidifier. (For more information on dehumidifiers, turn to page 52.)

If condensation is forming on pipes, cover them with adhesive-backed insulating tape or foam sleeve insulation, *opposite bottom*—both are affordable solutions and are available at home improvement stores.

Grades and gutters

Water-soaked soil pressing in on foundation walls is known as hydrostatic pressure. In some cases, the pressure is severe enough to crack concrete. While small cracks won't jeopardize the integrity of the foundation, they do provide water with an easy path inside. (To repair cracks, see the how-to illustrations, *opposite*.) Because both poured

REPAIR CRACKS

Use a cold chisel and a hammer to chisel minor cracks and holes, *right top*, so that they are wider at the bottom than they are at the top. This helps prevent the patch from popping out after it sets. Make the hole at least ½ inch deep. Then vacuum out any dust and concrete fragments.

Mix hydraulic cement in a bucket, adding water to the dry mix until it has a putty-like consistency. Then work it by hand. When plugging a hole, roll the mixture into the shape of a plug. For a crack, roll the hydraulic cement into a long, snake-like shape.

Press the material into the opening, *right bottom*. Keep working and applying pressure to the patch to make sure it fills every tiny crevice. Most cements will set even if water is leaking through the hole at the time of the repair (in which case, the water should stop running). Apply pressure to the patch for several minutes to allow it to set.

and block concrete walls are porous, they can wick water into the basement as well.

To solve either of these problems, route water away from the house so it doesn't collect around the foundation and seep inside. Make sure that the driveway, patios, sidewalks, and exposed earth slope away from the house. The grade should drop 2 inches vertically within one foot from the house. Continue this rate of decline for at least 3 feet to create a slope that drops 6 inches.

Another way to ensure that water doesn't soak in around a foundation is to check that gutters and downspouts are clear of debris and in good condition, with no sagging spots that can allow water to overflow. Add extensions, if necessary, to make sure that water is carried at least 5 feet away from the foundation.

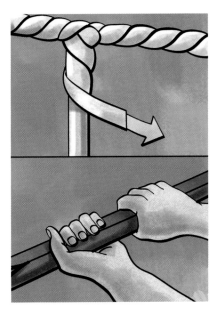

Specifically manufactured for covering pipes, insulating tape (top) and foam sleeve insulation (bottom) prevent humid air from condensing on pipe surfaces.

Water table woes

Occasionally a house is constructed in an area with a high water table—naturally occurring water that flows through soil like an underground river. With changing seasons, water tables fluctuate. When they are low, *below top*, a basement appears dry and problem-free. Under high pressure, a rising water table, *below bottom*, can force water up from below.

A thin, barely noticeable film of water on the basement floor is often the first sign of this problem. Test by laying down plastic sheeting for two days. Check for penetrating moisture that dampens the concrete underneath the plastic sheeting.

The best remedy for a high water table is to install a sump pump. (For more information on sump pumps, see page 52–53.) For added protection, you may also want to install an interior drainage system, *opposite*, that drains to a sump pump.

When the water table is low (above), basements are dry. When the table is high (below), such as after spring rains, moisture enters basements from several locations. A sump pump and/or an interior drainage system can help.

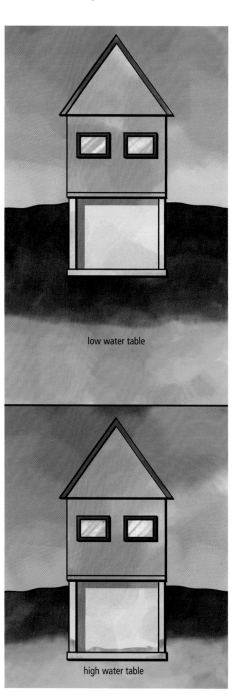

low water table

high water table

SEALERS: INSIDE AND OUT

When you occasionally discover damp spots in the basement, an interior cement-based sealer can help. Unfortunately sealers work only on bare concrete, so if your block or poured wall has been previously painted, you'll have to have the basement wall sealed on the exterior of the house.

To apply sealer inside on bare concrete, clean away dirt, grease, and dust from the walls using a stiff-bristle brush, *below top*. Thoroughly wet the wall with a fine mist from a garden hose. Mix liquid and powder components of a cement-based sealer according to manufacturer's directions and apply with a stiff brush.

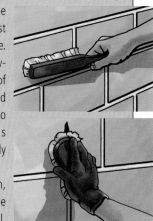

As you brush, *right*, fill in all the pores in the wall.

Go over cracks several times, if necessary, to fill them. If a crack is too large to fill with sealer, fill it first with hydraulic cement. Some sealers have to stay wet for several days to ensure bonding. Apply a second coat, if necessary.

Existing homes with extreme moisture problems may require exterior waterproofing—a costly proposition because dirt must be excavated away from the foundation to allow sealers and/or membranes to be applied to the walls. If you're building a new home, be sure to have exterior waterproofing applied before the contractor backfills soil.

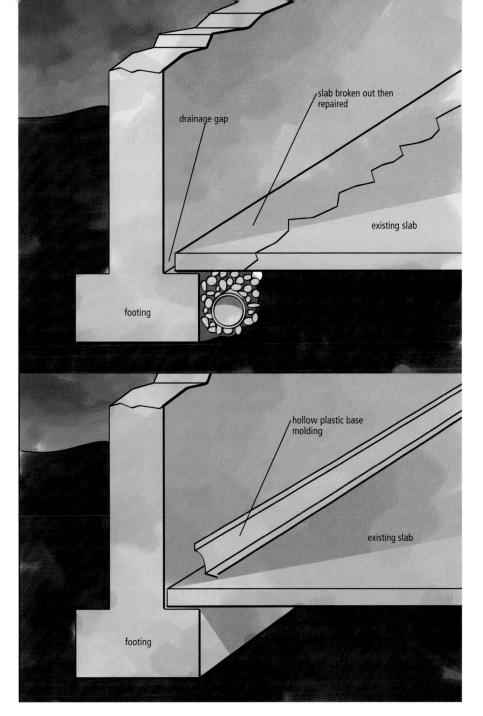

drainage gap

slab broken out then repaired

existing slab

footing

hollow plastic base molding

existing slab

footing

To install an interior-perimeter drainage system, you can remove the perimeter of the basement slab, dig a trench, fill it with gravel and a drainpipe that leads to a sump pump, then repair the slab (top). A less-invasive option is to glue a hollow plastic molding to the wall (bottom), which will trap water and channel it to a sump pump for removal.

Interior drainage systems

There are two types of interior drainage systems, which are also called dewatering systems. One requires a 1-foot-wide channel cut into the perimeter of the basement floor, all the way through the concrete. Perforated plastic drainpipe is fitted into the channel and covered with gravel. New concrete is then poured over the gravel to floor level. A slight space is left between the floor and the wall to allow weeping walls to drain directly into the channel. The drainpipe leads to a reservoir equipped with a sump pump. Excess water drains into the reservoir and is drawn outside the house by the sump pump.

Because this type of dewatering system is installed below floor level, it is sometimes effective in preventing problems caused by rising water tables.

The second type of dewatering system does not need an opening in the basement floor. Instead plastic channels are fixed to the basement walls with waterproof glue where the walls meet the floor, much like baseboard trim. The channels direct excess water to a sump pump location. Though adding plastic channels is less costly than opening the basement floor, it is not as effective at intercepting rising water tables as the below-floor system.

Wet Basement Rescue Checklist

Inspect your home's basement and foundation, using this checklist and the accompanying illustrations as a handy guide. As you identify potential trouble spots, follow through with the solutions to correct moisture issues.

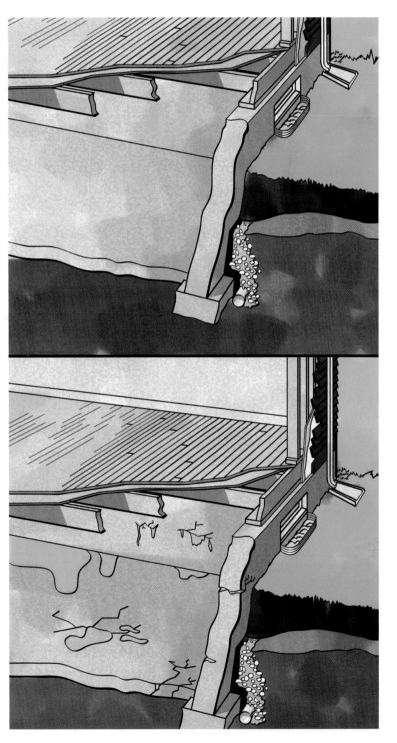

Six common problems

Investigate these potential problem areas around the foundation as well as the basement interior:

1 Gutters clogged and downspouts too short.

2 Windows positioned so close to soil level that water can enter.

3 Inadequate grading of soil near foundation walls.

4 High water table engulfs foundation.

5 Cracked walls.

6 Floor slab cracked by hydrostatic pressure.

To resolve the problems, *left bottom*, try these suggestions:

■ **Clean gutters and extend downspouts (or add splash blocks).** Debris collecting inside gutters can dam downspouts, causing water to overflow and end up next to the foundation. Clean them in the spring and fall to avoid problems. Make sure all gutters are straight and slope gently toward downspout locations. Sagging gutters trap water in low spots and cause overflowing. Downspouts should extend at least 5 feet from foundation walls. Lengthen short downspouts or place concrete splash blocks beneath downspout openings to direct water away from foundation walls.

■ **Install window wells** (see pages 38–39, 49). According to building codes, the outside bottom edge of a basement window should be at least 6 inches above the soil to prevent leakage from groundwater and to keep wood framing members from rotting.

■ **Add or remove soil to achieve the proper grade slope.** To prevent moisture damage to the basement interior, soil should slope downward 6 vertical inches for a distance of 3 horizontal feet.

■ **Install a perimeter drainage system to carry away excess water** (see page 31). An interior drainage system, or dewatering system, intercepts water where foundation walls meet the floor. From that point, water is directed to a sump pump (see pages 52–53) so it can be removed.

■ **Fill cracks in walls** (see page 29) **and apply sealer** (see page 30). The pressure of water-soaked soil cracks basement walls. The damage usually occurs during colder months when water-laden soil freezes and expands, pushing against basement walls with enough force to crack masonry. If you see a crack line running horizontally across the basement wall, it may be that builders poured part of the wall and allowed it to harden before pouring the rest. In this case, have the crack inspected by an engineer.

■ **Fill cracks in the floor** (use the same techniques and materials for filling cracks in walls on page 29) **and apply sealer** (see page 30). First gauge the severity of the cracks, and follow the guidelines on page 34 to determine the best remedy.

Floor Fixups

After you solve moisture problems, your main concern becomes the basement floor: Is it sound and level enough to finish with your floor covering choice? If your floor shows no signs of moisture problems, is level (no high spots of more than $\frac{1}{8}$ inch in 10 feet), and is not severely cracked, it may need only surface repairs before you install underlayment (in areas you intend to cover with vinyl) or a finished floor. If it's badly cracked, broken, or damaged, you'll have to resurface it, either with self-leveling compound or new cement.

First check the floor's surface for evenness by rotating a 6-foot level on the floor in sections. Mark dips or high spots with a carpenter's pencil. Repair those areas as follows:

Lows and highs. Fill depressions with patching compound, troweling them smooth and feathering them to the surrounding floor. Rent a concrete grinder to level high spots. Check the surface of your repairs with a straightedge, continuing to fill or grind until the floor is flat and level.

Cracks and holes. Use hydraulic cement to repair, as described on page 29.

Salt deposits. White or yellow alkaline deposits impair adhesive bonding on glued-down floor coverings. To remove them, mop the floor with a solution of four parts water and one part muriatic acid; then rinse the slab with clean water. Muriatic acid is extremely caustic, so follow package directions carefully.

If your floor is extensively damaged and can't be repaired using these techniques—or if such repairs would be too time-consuming—you still have two more options for making a lasting repair. Before you choose either, though, consult a structural engineer to determine the cause of your floor's damage and to ensure that its condition is stable enough that it won't sustain more damage.

Self-leveling compound is a liquid mortar that you pour and spread onto a sloped, rough, uneven, but structurally sound floor. Most compounds require that you first coat the floor with a primer. After the primer has cured, you mix the compound and spread it onto the floor—up to $\frac{1}{2}$ inch thick—with a floor squeegee. The compound levels itself and dries hard and smooth. If you need a thickness greater than $\frac{1}{2}$ inch, add aggregate to the mix.

If your floor is not structurally sound, you don't have to break up the old slab and start again. You can pour a new slab right over the old one as long as the increase in floor height leaves you enough headroom (consult your local building codes for minimum ceiling height requirements). First install any new plumbing. Then lay a waterproof membrane—such as 6-mil polyethylene plastic sheeting—over the old slab as a moisture barrier, overlapping edges by at least 4 inches. Then lay $\frac{1}{2}$-inch rigid foam around the perimeter of the floor as an expansion barrier, and suspend 6×6-inch #10 wire mesh on brick or pieces of block to center the wire in the concrete when it is poured. Pour at least 4 inches of concrete and finish it with a float.

Opposite: **A sound basement floor will allow you to finish your basement with nearly any material you choose. This child's playroom takes a creative turn with tightly woven black olefin carpet inset with a black-and-white checkerboard, bordered in red, for game-playing fun.**

Crack the Codes

The good news is you don't have to become intimate with your local building codes to plan your basement remodeling. The even better news is that your local building official is there to help you achieve what you want from your project and obtain a building permit.

Building codes are specifically designed to protect the structural integrity of your home as well as remove potential threats to your health and safety. For your first visit with the building official, be prepared to describe your project—even if your ideas are rough—and ask what building codes would apply in your situation.

Bring along a rough sketch of the available basement space—as well as the location and dimensions of all windows, doors, and mechanical systems—to make your visit even more productive. Don't be discouraged if local codes call for a standard that you apparently can't meet. If safety or practicality isn't compromised, many building officials are willing to make exceptions to accommodate existing homes.

For example, you may discover from building officials that the International Residential Code requires basement rooms to have a minimum ceiling height of 7 feet (84 inches) over at least 50 percent of the floor area. Bathrooms, hallways, and task

PLAN AHEAD
If you're building a new house, boost your home's value from the get-go by having your builder dig a foundation for a 9- or 10-foot ceiling instead of the standard 7 or 8. The extra cost is nominal. Even if you don't finish the basement, your home's future owners will appreciate the headroom and the potential that it yields. If you like that idea, bypass the standard basement windows from the start, too, and install egress windows.

areas can have ceilings that dip as low as 76 inches in some locations.

Armed with this information, you can find out if you have enough room to create a new living area. Simply measure the distance between the floor and the bottom of the ceiling joists. Subtract a couple of inches from your figures to allow for finished floor and ceiling materials.

Other elements are governed by codes, such as the requirement that a smoke detector be installed in every sleeping room and in hallways leading to them. Carbon monoxide detectors are not required by code, but it's a good idea to install one near all sleeping areas. Better yet, place one next to the smoke detector in every bedroom. Building

Room Size Recommendations

The U.S. Department of Housing and Urban Development recommends the following sizes for specific rooms.

Minimum net floor area is within enclosed walls (excluding built-in features, such as cabinets and closets).

ROOM	MIN AREA (square feet)	MIN SIZE (feet)	PREFERRED (feet)
Master Bedroom	n/a	n/a	12x16
Bedroom	80	8x10	11x14
Family Room	110	10.5x10.5	12x16
Living Room	176	11x16	12x18
Great Room	n/a	n/a	14x20
Bathroom	35	5x7	5x9

codes also govern construction materials for fire safety.

Kitchens and baths and the features that go with them have their own sets of codes, so discuss those with the building official, too. Here are a few other general features that you'll probably want to discuss with your building official:

■ **Stairs.** Tread, riser, and headroom measurements, plus handrail shape and location. (See page 40 for more information on stairs.)

■ **General construction.** Lumber specifications, stud and joist spacing, nail and screw types and spacing.

■ **Mechanicals.** Electric cable type, number and placement of receptacles; ground-fault circuit interrupters (GFIs); plumbing pipe material (copper, plastic, steel) and size, solder type, venting, traps, and connections.

Finally, the I-codes—a coordinated, comprehensive set of building codes that serve the nation—maintain that habitable rooms must measure at least 7×7 feet. That's a pretty tiny room. Take a look at the recommendations, *opposite,* for a better idea of appropriate measurements.

Despite the attractive coffered ceiling treatment in this basement game room, ductwork and pipes hang as low as they do in ordinary basements— they're simply worked into the design. Your local building official can help you with ceiling height minimums as well as the other standards in your local codes.

Ways with Windows and Doors

Even if it's dim in your basement right now, your future could be bright, cheerful, and more accessible by adding windows and doors or enlarging existing windows. As you evaluate your basement for window and door needs, find out what you need to do to meet local codes. (See "Window Requirements," *opposite*.)

If your foundation is entirely below grade, you can dig a window well to accommodate a larger window—an option that pulls in nearly as much light as one located above grade. Your window well can be 12 inches deep or more and as wide as you want. Retain the soil surrounding the well with a ready-made steel insert or use more attractive materials, such as limestone blocks or the painted cement blocks used in the well, *right*. Scenic vistas, printed on weather-resistant polystyrene, *opposite top*, are also available to create a "view."

Greenhouse-type windows atop a basement bump-out, *below*, are another option, and do an especially good job of scooping in natural light.

To capture morning light, place windows facing east. For all-day exposure, point them south. West-facing windows obviously will pull in warmer afternoon sun—something to avoid in warmer climates.

If you're fortunate enough to own a house with a walk-out basement, you already may enjoy the benefits of good access and light pouring into the space through a patio door, *opposite bottom*. For foundations situated partially or entirely below grade, you can explore the feasibility of excavating soil to create a walkout. Consult an engineer, an architect, or a qualified builder to find out if your space allows this option.

Building codes require windows with wells deeper than 44 inches to be fitted with steps or a ladder. This approach cleverly transforms the steps into a garden until they're needed for escape.

Greenhouse windows installed over a basement bump-out fill a below-grade space with light. To see the interior, turn to page 48.

BASEMENT BASICS

For quick access from the outside to a basement storage area or workshop, install bulkhead doors, which are set at an angle to the foundation and open to a staircase. The doors lift to open—much like doors once used to enter a farmhouse storm shelter or fruit cellar.

WINDOW REQUIREMENTS

One important common aspect of building codes is window requirements. Habitable rooms must have window square footage that measures 8 percent of the room's total square footage. For ventilation, half the window square footage amount must be operable. For example, a 100-square-foot room measuring 10×10 feet requires 8 square feet of windows with 4 square feet of operable area. If the ventilation requirement can't be met with windows, then doors, louvers, vents, and even mechanical devices—such as a furnace vent—can be used. Remember your building official will need to agree on sufficient provisions.

For safe exits in the event of fire, all sleeping rooms above or below grade are required to have either a door to the outside or a window with 5.7 square feet of operable area through which a person can escape. Window wells that are 44 inches below grade level must have a permanent ladder or steps. Building code standards aside, it makes good sense to provide plenty of safe exists whether a room is intended for sleeping or not.

A decorative window well liner conceals an unattractive corrugated steel liner while creating the illusion of a view. A number of "views" are available to suit the setting or your imagination.

A walk-out basement allows the installation of a patio door and easy access to the yard. If your foundation is entirely below grade, consider excavating soil away to create a walkout (consult an engineer or architect) or excavate a patio-size well lined with stone or cement block (see page 49).

Stepping In

Opposite: Stairs with a small landing lead to this basement. Rather than let the angled space beneath the landing and stairs go to waste, these niches put the space to work storing the television, DVD player, and stereo equipment. For a better look at these media niches and for more ideas on putting under-stair space to work, see page 58.

You already have stairs to your basement, of course, but now is a good time to make sure they meet code. (See "Stair Codes," *below,* and also speak with your building official.) You'll also want to consider how the basement stairs contribute to the space in terms of looks and convenience. If your steps don't measure up to code or if the location in the basement won't allow you to sensibly arrange the room, you can rebuild them and even relocate them if it would better serve both upper-level and lower-level living areas. (See "Stair-Positioning Tips," *opposite.*)

Codes vary with stair configurations and railing shape, so you'll need to talk to the building official about these as well. It's also a good idea to talk to an architect or other design professional to make sure that the stairway style works well with your other ideas. Here are some of the stair designs, shown in the illustration *below,* for you to consider:

■ Straight-run stairs take up about 40 square feet of floor space at the lower level.

■ L- or U-shape stairs require more floor area but are a good choice when a straight run is too steep.

■ Spiral stairs are usually only 4 to 6 feet in diameter, so they take up little floor space. If you consider this option, you'll need another route for moving furniture and other large objects into the basement (such as a walk-out access). Building codes often prohibit spiral stairs leading to rooms larger than 400 square feet.

■ Winder staircases eliminate the need for a landing around a sharp turn.

STAIR CODES

Here are typical building code requirements for a basic "straight run" of stairs leading to habitable rooms.

Riser height	4-inch minimum, 8-inch maximum
Tread depth	9-inch minimum
Handrail	34 to 38 inches above tread
Balusters	Spaced so that a 3-inch sphere can't pass between posts
Headroom	80-inch minimum

- Locate stairs where people won't have to walk through a bedroom or bath to reach a main living area.
- Place stairs leading to family rooms and recreation rooms near the kitchen.
- Avoid connecting noisy rooms to quiet ones. If it can't be avoided, soundproof the stairwell by insulating the walls that surround it.
- Stairs built parallel to ceiling joists take less time to install and require fewer cuts and fewer materials than stairs built perpendicular to ceiling joists.

Increase Comfort

After your basement is dry, the floors and walls are repaired and sealed, and you've planned for windows, doors, and the stairway, you need to consider other mechanical elements to make the lower level as comfortable as possible.

Heating and cooling

Basements are usually cool year-round—comfortably so in summer, a bit chilly in winter. Basements are often partially insulated by the ground around them, so your existing heating system should provide the

moderate amount of heat needed to bring them up to comfortable temperatures. It's always a good idea, though, to make your basement even more energy efficient by wrapping walls in insulation with R-10 to R-19 values.

Your current cooling system probably does a sufficient job of keeping the basement comfortable during the hottest summer days. If you're having difficulty keeping a walk-out basement cool in summer, consult a heating and cooling contractor to determine whether you need a more powerful

One way to make a basement more comfortable is to include a gas fireplace for warmth, such as the one in this lower-level family room. Fireplaces can be an eye-catching architectural focal point too.

cooling system. You also could consider supplementing the current system with a window air-conditioner.

Many basements in homes cooled and heated by forced air already have the ductwork necessary to distribute the warmed or cooled air. If not, a technician can install ductwork relatively simply and inexpensively because a furnace is usually located on the lower level. Still your basement may need a supplemental heat source. If you have a walk-out basement with large, unshaded, south-facing windows, you may need supplemental cooling as well.

If modifying or expanding the main heating and cooling system in your home is impractical, you still have options. In fact, some of the products listed may prove more efficient, especially if you will not be using your new space constantly.

■ **Electric heaters** of all kinds are usually the easiest and least costly to install but are the most expensive to operate. Electric heat still can be an efficient and comfortable solution, however, especially if you live in a mild climate, heat only sporadically, or heat only a small area.

■ **Baseboard heaters** are 4 or 6 feet long and operate on normal household electrical current. Plug them into a wall outlet or hard-wire them to an electrical circuit. Baseboard heaters are quiet and easy to conceal, but again, they are also more costly and ineffective in larger areas.

■ **Electric wall heaters** feature built-in fans to distribute heat and are small enough to fit in confined spaces, such as bathrooms. Because of the fans, wall heaters distribute heat faster but make some noise. They also must be hard-wired into your home's circuits. Consider furniture placement when

you locate a wall heater to avoid blocking the fan.

■ **Portable heaters** come in several varieties: radiant heaters, which produce instant warmth; oil-filled radiators, which produce a quiet, even heat; and ceramic heaters, which are powerful yet compact. These heaters allow you to heat just the area you're using and are an efficient way to keep comfortable if you don't use your new space for long periods of time. The newest ceramic heaters use an electronic temperature control to smoothly vary the output of both the heating element and a very quiet fan. Their small size and ability to hold a constant temperature without cycling on and off make these units popular. Be sure to purchase only a new heater and look for one that has an oxygen depletion sensor, which will automatically shut off the unit before building up a hazardous atmosphere.

■ **Direct-vent gas heaters** are efficient, quiet, thermostatically controlled units that provide plenty of clean heat. They're designed to heat a room's air and then distribute the heated air with a fan. A pipe exits the rear of the appliance and penetrates an exterior wall to vent exhaust gases and draw combustion air into the appliance.

Beyond traditional heating systems, you can consider other options to make your basement a warm, dry, and more welcoming place:

All fired up

Fireplaces not only make a room more inviting, but when chosen wisely, they can make it warmer during cold seasons.

Wood heat from most wood-burning fireplaces sucks more hot air out of a room than it produces, so these fireplaces are valued more for their ambience. Airtight, wood-burning stoves—some that allow you to see the fire—can be a great way to heat your new space, especially if you have a good source of wood to burn. They require lighting, stoking, ash cleaning, and the carrying in and out of messy fuel, though, so they're not for everyone.

Direct-vent gas fireplaces allow you to see the flames and be warmed by their radiant heat. Some include a fan to distribute warmed air as well, making them efficient as well as decorative. Regardless of the style you choose, you'll find them available in a variety of looks, sizes, heat output levels, and prices. Plan to connect a direct-vent gas fire-

This direct-vent gas fireplace offers power-assisted venting—a fan inside the vent helps exhaust combustion byproducts.

place to existing gas lines; LP-fired models are also available. These units offer a combination of aesthetics, efficiency, safety, and ease of installation. They're vented to the outdoors with a short length of two-in-one pipe that carries combustion byproducts out and draws in fresh air for combustion. The pipe can make two right-angle turns without losing any efficiency. You can choose a fireplace that's freestanding or ready for framing; its function may be more decorative or one that's intended to provide heat. A major advantage of having a gas fireplace in your home is that if your power fails, it can provide some heat (and some provide quite a lot—check the BTU output ratings of the units you're considering).

Ventless (also called vent-free) gas fireplaces exhaust combustion byproducts directly into the room. They're slightly more efficient than direct-vent units and are even easier to install, but they deplete the room's oxygen supply, produce fumes that can be a health hazard, and are more risky for basement spaces. Some states have banned their use. Most of today's ventless gas fireplaces are required to include an oxygen depletion sensor (ODS), a safety feature that warns if oxygen levels in the room are becoming low. For health reasons, you're much better off with a direct-vent appliance.

A warmer floor

If you plan to finish your basement floor with stone or tile, consider installing a radiant heating system first. These heating systems not only warm the floor, they also increase the overall temperature of the room, often eliminating the need for additional heaters. (For more information about radiant heating systems, see page 53.)

You can either install a radiant heating system yourself—they are available at most home centers—or you can hire a flooring professional to install the system for you.

For rooms where you plan to use other finish flooring materials, such as carpeting, consider installing a wood subfloor with sleepers (floor joists that rest directly on the

concrete floor). Use sleepers to protect a floor from condensation or as an alternative to a liquid leveler when you don't want to fix cracks, tilts, or imperfections. You can also install sleepers if you want to insulate the floor. You must install a wood subfloor if your finished floor is the kind that has to be

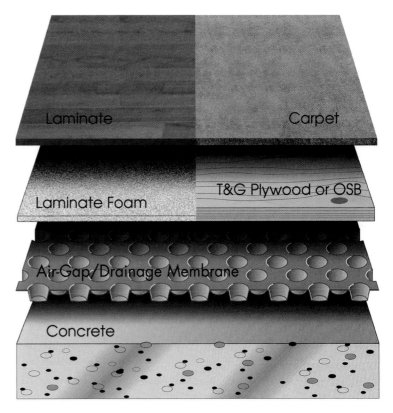

Laminate

Carpet

Laminate Foam

T&G Plywood or OSB

Air-Gap/Drainage Membrane

Concrete

nailed down. (For more on flooring materials, turn to pages 52–53.)

Another option for installing warmer, drier floors is to cover the concrete first with a special air-gap/drainage membrane—an option that can cost 40 to 50 percent less than a wood subfloor. This dimpled plastic membrane acts as a barrier between the concrete and whatever finish flooring you choose, *above,* blocking out damp and cold. The dimples offer cushion and create a continuous air gap over the surface of the concrete, which serves as insulation. The gap also allows concrete to breathe and dry by permitting any airborne moisture to be vented to the wall.

Air-gap/drainage membrane comes in 4×8-foot sheets that are laid over the concrete surface and cut to allow a ¼-inch space between the wall and floorboard. The space allows for expansion and air flow beneath the floor. Most floating hardwood floors and laminate floors can be installed directly over the membrane. By topping the membrane with plywood, you can install tile, vinyl, or carpet.

Shape the Space

With your basement ready for finishing, it's time to focus your ideas and claim the additional living space now within your reach.

Opposite: French doors provide an elegant entry to this home office where pickled cabinets are as practical as they are pleasing to look at. Including cabinets in your basement floor plan increases storage and provides space to display your treasures as well as an array of audiovisual equipment.

By now you've probably spent many hours sketching floor plan ideas on everything from napkins to the back of the grocery list. It's time to boil those thoughts down to a few favorites and plan more precisely. The grid paper, templates, and guidelines that wrap up this chapter will help you through this step.

You'll also find information on constructing non-load-bearing walls as well as ways to soundproof ceilings and walls. Also look over the options for finishing the walls, floors, and ceilings; try to imagine your rooms as they would appear with these materials. Do the ones you're considering match your lifestyle and decorating tastes?

As you plan the layout, experiment with the myriad options for storage. Finishing the basement is the ideal time to make your household more organized, and well-planned closets and cabinetry will help you clear clutter.

Finally use the information for dehumidifiers and sump pumps to help sort through the details and make the best choice. Think of these helpful devices as insurance to keep your basement dry and comfortable.

ENERGY EFFICIENCY

Look for the following criteria when buying windows. In each case, the lower the value, the more energy-efficient the window:

U-VALUES. The National Fenestration Rating Council (NFRC) rates the windows of participating manufacturers for the amount of heat that flows through a product (its U-value).

SOLAR HEAT GAIN COEFFICIENCY (SHGC) reflects the amount of energy that passes from the exterior to the interior, and air leakage.

ENERGY STAR. To quickly identify good performers, the Energy Star program, a voluntary partnership between the U.S. Department of Energy and participating manufacturers, gives its seal of approval to windows with a U-value of 0.35 or lower, and an SHGC rating of 0.40 or lower.

Windows

Inviting sunshine into your basement can be one of the most rewarding parts of the planning process. The daylight filters in to make the rooms more welcoming. Your options include either replacing small existing windows with larger units or installing additional windows.

If you're including a bedroom in your basement remodeling plans, remember that this room must have an egress opening (see "Window Requirements," page 39). If you want to add an egress opening, examine the area immediately outside the proposed window location for obstructions. Consider privacy, too. If the new window will be close to sidewalks or another house, you can use a fence, wall, or plantings to screen the area.

Adding or enlarging basement windows is not a job for the average do-it-yourselfer. It involves removing portions of the foundation wall and supporting the structure above the wall opening with a header constructed of two or more 2× lengths of lumber. These span the opening and carry the weight of the house. Cutting concrete or concrete block and maintaining structural integrity are tasks best left to an experienced professional.

Most building codes require the outside bottom edge of the new window to be at least 6 inches above the soil to prevent groundwater from leaking in and to keep wood framing members from rotting. The space between the bottom of the header and a point 6 inches above the soil line should be big enough to install a window unit at least

To create this basement sunroom, a greenhouse bump-out takes advantage of a generous amount of above-grade wall area. The bottoms of the windows are just above the soil. To see the exterior view of this bump-out, turn to page 38 (below).

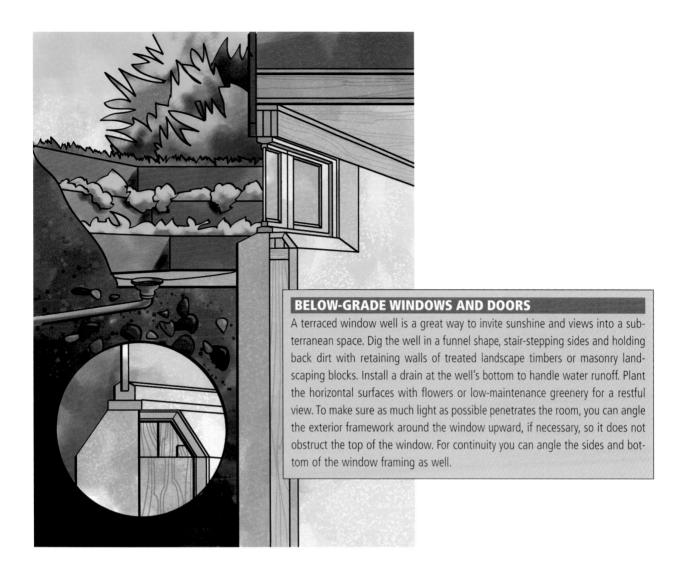

1 foot high. This is a minimum standard, however, and increasing the size of the window will bring in more light.

Window openings that extend below grade must have a window well, *above*. Installing a window well requires excavating the soil outside foundation walls and installing a retaining wall of galvanized steel or masonry. The floor of the well must have a drainage system, preferably a gravel bed and a drainpipe connected to a perimeter drain. If there is no perimeter drain, the gravel bed must be approximately 6 inches deep to hold precipitation until it seeps into the surrounding soil. Install rigid foam insulation between the gravel bed and the foundation to encourage water to migrate away from the wall.

Take the idea of a window well a step further and create a below-grade patio with a sliding door that brings in an abundance of light. A well such as this doesn't take much space but is roomy enough for a collection of plants or a small grill.

The best time to add architectural interest to a typical rectangular basement is during the framing stage. A short, irregular stud wall gives three-dimensional shape to an otherwise plain basement wall.

Walls

Help make your basement living space quieter with products such as acoustic wall framing that reduces noise transmission through interior walls; a floor mat to isolate noise from entertainment systems and appliances; and caulk. Use acoustic fiberglass batts in interior walls, under floors, and above ceilings.

Foundation walls are usually made of poured concrete or stacked concrete block—not the most attractive surfaces. Fortunately you can cover basement walls quickly and inexpensively. Attach wood furring strips, Z-shape channels, or 2×4 studs to flat, dry masonry walls, then add insulation and cover the strips or studs with drywall. Such treatments give walls a smooth, even surface that accepts finish materials, such as paint, wallpaper, or paneling. This type of wall system makes it easy to install electrical wiring, television cable, speaker wire, and telephone lines.

If basement walls are bowed or out-of-plumb, build a stud wall in front of them to ensure a flat, plumb, finished wall surface. (See "Button Up Bows," page 28.) In this case, the stud wall is not attached to the masonry wall. Just like a partition wall (see the illustration, *opposite*), the top plate is attached to overhead joists and the bottom plate is nailed to the concrete slab.

To make your basement more energy efficient, fill the spaces between the furring strips with rigid insulation. Or fill spaces between 2×4 studs with fiberglass batt insulation. In cold climates, you may want to include a vapor barrier during the insulation process. The vapor barrier, typically either separate plastic sheeting or treated paper attached to one side of the fiberglass batt, is designed to prevent warmed air from condensing inside the cooler insulation. You should not install a vapor barrier in warmer climates because moisture moves both into and out of the house for significant portions of the year.

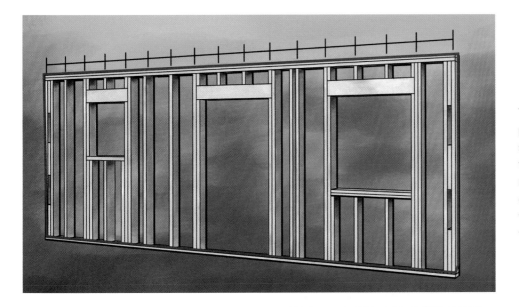

The bottom plate of the partition wall should be secured to the basement floor with 2-inch masonry nails or a ½-inch bead of construction adhesive. The top plate should be nailed to the ceiling joists.

Partition walls

Because partition walls don't have to support the weight of the house, they are easy to construct and install in virtually any basement location to create separate rooms. This versatility also makes them ideal for camouflaging posts and other obstructions that can't be moved.

Typical stud wall construction is sufficient for partition walls, but don't stifle your creative instincts. Curved walls or walls made of glass block are simple ways to enhance a basement. Also, you can open a windowless room to other areas of the basement by adding a window to an interior partition wall, such as the one in the basement office shown on page 7.

Be sure to insulate partition stud walls that define noisier spaces—such as the laundry room or home theater—or private spaces, such as an office or bedroom, following the guidelines below.

BASEMENT BASICS

Boost your basement's energy efficiency to save on heating and cooling costs by insulating the outside walls. Rigid foam panels do the job best. Foam offers more insulating value than fiberglass batts in less space. Foam is also ideal when paired with masonry; it's impervious to moisture and water, and can be covered with drywall, without studs.

SOUNDS OF SILENCE

Building materials are getting lighter, but that makes them more prone to transmitting noise than blocking it. To control sound, try these strategies:

• For partition walls, apply a bead of silicone caulk to the front edge of 2x4 studs and top with a sheet of drywall. Secure the drywall to the stud using nails or screws. To this drywall sheet, apply additional beads of caulk that align with each stud. Apply a second sheet of drywall. This second sheet, along with the caulk, helps dampen sound.

• In lieu of two layers of drywall, install acoustical fiberglass batts within interior walls and ceilings, especially around noise sources, such as laundry rooms, bathrooms, and media centers.

• Caulk floor, wall, and ceiling edges. Noise can escape through joints where walls meet floors and the ceiling.

• Other noise-reduction building products are also available, such as acoustical wall framing, floor mats, and acoustical caulk.

• Adding textiles to your room also can help absorb sound. Carpeting, fabric on walls, and even upholstered furnishings diminish noise transmission.

Floors

Unless you install a plywood subfloor (see the subhead, "Subfloor Alternative," *opposite*), your basement floor is most likely a concrete slab. You can apply or install many kinds of flooring materials over concrete for an attractive, durable finish.

Carpet

The softness and warmth of carpeting makes it ideal for basement living spaces because it cushions the hard concrete surface below. Installing carpet over concrete is easy—perimeter tack strips specifically manufactured for concrete hold the carpet in place. After you've solved basement dampness problems, you shouldn't have to worry about moisture getting trapped underneath. For an extra measure of protection, seal the concrete with urethane concrete sealer or concrete paint before installing carpet. Or try a membrane product, such as the one shown on page 45. Be sure to choose a rubber pad—

foam pads may deteriorate with prolonged exposure to humid conditions.

Ceramic tile

Ceramic tile—available in many styles and colors—is durable, beautiful, and installs easily over concrete. One drawback of ceramic tile in a basement is that it tends to stay cool, especially during winter. Consider installing a radiant heat system beneath the flooring to maintain a warmer surface. (See "Warmth Underfoot," *opposite*.)

Vinyl

For a tough, cost-effective floor covering, consider vinyl sheeting or vinyl tiles. These are easily glued to concrete subfloors. Cushion-backed sheet vinyl offers an extra measure of comfort over hard concrete slabs. For any vinyl product, make sure the subfloor is completely smooth and free of defects before installation. Otherwise, imperfections, such as cracks, eventually will

---

DEWATERING DEVICES

Part of maintaining the comfort of your basement is making sure it stays dry. A dehumidifier and a sump pump are two devices that can do that for you.

Dehumidifiers are rated by how much they can dehumidify and how many pints of water per hour they can remove from the air. Know the square footage of your basement before you buy, and make sure you purchase an appliance that has enough capacity to do the job. Most units are automatic and can be set either to run continuously or maintain a preset humidity level—a convenient feature. The units have removable basins or buckets to catch the water—most with a knockout at the bottom where you can attach a tube or hose that can run directly into a floor drain. Otherwise you need to remember to empty the machine periodically. Dehumidifiers remove moisture from the air that can cause condensation, mold, and mildew. They work best if the source of moisture comes from within the house—from using a bath or shower or washing clothes, for example—and do nothing to prevent water from entering the room.

Sump pumps are rated according to how many gallons of water per minute they can pump and how high they can lift the water. Battery-powered sump pumps work during short power outages—a must if short, violent storms often cause your basement to flood. Twice a year, check that the battery is charged. Most sump pumps exhaust water through a plastic pipe buried in a shallow trench in your yard. The pipe then carries the water to a street gutter where it flows into a storm drain or to a distant low spot on your property. Connecting a sump pump to a sewer line is not recommended (and not allowed by some local codes). It can overload the sewer line, especially in homes with septic systems.

show through the flooring and possibly cause the material to tear.

Laminate

Laminate flooring features a decorative image printed on one or more thin sheets of paper or other fibrous material. The decorative layer, which mimics a variety of materials such as wood, ceramic tile, or stone, is impregnated with plastic or resin and bonded to a rigid core for durability. Today's virtually stain-proof laminate planks or tiles are easy to clean, never fade, and never need waxing. Add pads to furniture feet to avoid scratching the flooring surface.

Engineered wood vs. wood flooring

People are most familiar with wood flooring as solid, one-piece boards. Most solid wood flooring is not recommended for below-grade installations because it can shrink and expand, resulting in gaps or warping. As an attractive alternative, consider engineered wood, which consists of two or more layers of wood laminated together—similar to plywood but not to be confused with laminate flooring. The top, or wear layer, is hardwood veneer, and the lower layers are usually softwood. It is usually suitable for below-grade installations because it shrinks and expands less than solid wood flooring.

Subfloor alternative

For comfort underfoot or to span an uneven concrete slab, install a wooden subfloor. In a typical installation, ⅝- or ¾-inch exterior-grade plywood sheets are nailed to a grid of "sleepers"—pressure-treated 2×4s laid flat to help keep the finished height within the 90 inches required by building codes. Correct any unevenness in the concrete by placing shims beneath the sleepers. Fill spaces between the sleepers with rigid foam insulation before nailing the plywood in

place. The result is a smooth, even subfloor that will accept most types of flooring.

Warmth underfoot

Radiant heating systems installed between the subfloor and the finish floor usually have a network of electrical heating cables or tubes to hold hot water. Most systems can be installed across the entire floor—such as the family room or home theater where people like to camp out on the floor—or confined to a specific area such as in the bathroom in front of a vanity or bathtub. Like other heating systems, radiant heating is controlled by a thermostat that can be turned on or off, up or down.

You can either install a radiant heating system yourself—they are available at most home centers and are surprisingly affordable—or you can hire a flooring professional to install the system for you.

A sump pump draws water out of a sump— a hole beneath the basement floor—so the basement doesn't flood. Combined with tight walls and floors, and a dehumidifier, it keeps your basement pleasantly dry.

Ceilings

Finishing the basement ceiling sometimes calls for a little creative thinking as you figure out how to conceal ductwork, pipes, and other obstructions. You can usually move wires and water supply pipes, but finding acceptable new routes for ductwork or drain lines often is difficult. One option is to disguise or box in obstructions within a wood framework, then cover the frame with finish materials.

The three primary options for finishing basement ceilings are hanging drywall or wood (such as beaded board or tongue-and-groove siding), installing a suspended ceiling, or simply painting the joists. Another option is to attach fabric panels to joists.

Drywall

Drywall creates a smooth, even ceiling and helps give a basement the look of main-floor living areas. However, drywall does inhibit quick access to faulty wiring or a leaking pipe. It is an excellent base for paint and other materials, such as wood panels. For safety, some building codes require that you install drywall under flammable materials,

The exposed ceiling joists, wires, and pipes in this basement pool room are hidden by a coat of brown paint. Using an airless sprayer to apply the paint makes quick work of this finishing option.

The ceiling of the child's playroom shown on page 9 features fabric stapled to overhead joists and draped in billowy folds. The result is a simple, cost-effective covering that hides pipes, wires, and ductwork.

such as wood, because of the fire-retardant quality of drywall.

While you can relocate some pipes and wires so they aren't in the way, you will have to box in large obstructions, such as ducts and drain pipes, with a wood framework. Although obstructions are unavoidable, careful planning will ensure that any boxed-in elements become an integral part of your finished basement.

Suspended ceilings

A low-cost, low-maintenance option is to install a drop or suspended ceiling system. Though these systems have been given a bad name for years, there are now a number of attractive options available, including styles that mimic materials such as decorative tin or wood. This system includes a framework of metal channels hung on wires attached to the joists. (However, some types of ceiling panels are secured directly to joists.) The channels support lightweight acoustical panels that form a uniform finished surface. The suspended ceiling system has several advantages for basement applications. Moving wires, pipes, or ducts is unnecessary, and joists do not have to be straight for the finished ceiling to be flat and level. Accessing heating, cooling, or electrical systems is a simple matter of temporarily removing a panel. You can add lighting by removing an acoustical panel and fitting the opening with a drop-in fixture made specifically for the purpose. Suspended ceilings have the added benefit of insulating unwanted noise from upstairs.

Painting

One low-cost finishing option is to leave all the elements in the ceiling exposed but camouflage the overhead tangle with paint. Painting everything a single color blends the different elements together and creates a look that evokes industrial style or a fun and funky decor. A paint sprayer will coat everything evenly—including the sides and much of the upper surfaces of various elements. Paint the joists, the underside of the subfloor, wires, pipes, and ducts. Both light and dark colors work well. Dark colors disguise the many elements better while light colors help make the space brighter.

Plan Storage

High on any homeowner's list of desired features is plenty of organized storage, and the basement can yield an abundance of such specialized storage opportunities. So don't commit every inch of the basement floor space to new living area. The illustrations, *opposite,* show absolute minimum dimensions for conventional and walk-in closets. Build enough storage space to hold everything you need to store in the room you're creating, plus everything you currently store in the unfinished space. A full wall of shelving and cabinetry, attractively arranged around a media center or fireplace, is one high-capacity solution. Another is to reserve a small room for storage only. Wire shelving is easy to install in a variety of configurations that include special features such as drawers or shoe organizers.

CEDAR CLOSETS MAKE SCENTS

To repel moths and other fabric-noshing bugs, store woolens, quilts, furs, and off-season clothing in a cedar closet you install in the basement.

The sweet aroma emitted by orange-red heartwood cedar is one of nature's perfumes to humans, but it repels moths and other insects. Without this scent to keep them away, adult moths can invade your best sweaters and blankets and lay eggs in the fabrics. When the eggs hatch into larvae, the larvae feed on the fabrics, leaving behind undesirable pea-size holes.

Set aside one closet area and plan to line it with tongue-and-groove cedar strips, which cost about $1.25 to $1.85 per square foot. Then add closet hanging poles and wire bins and shelves for storing items.

Although not as effective as cedar lining in repelling pests, cedar shelves or cedar hanging poles offer a lower cost alternative to a fully lined closet.

Clad in rich blue laminate, these vibrant laundry room cabinets offer abundant storage. Doubling as a sewing space, the room features the usual laundry facilities and sink, plus two sewing machines and a refrigerator for beverages and snacks.

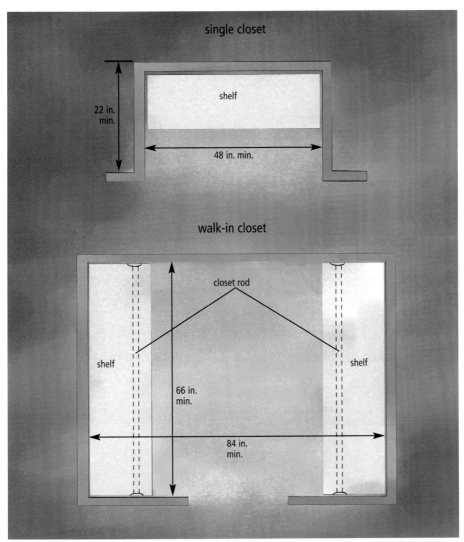

single closet

shelf

22 in. min.

48 in. min.

walk-in closet

closet rod

shelf

shelf

66 in. min.

84 in. min.

The illustrations show a top view and minimum dimensions for conventional and walk-in closets. Put every inch of that vertical space to work by grouping your items by size and placing them on shelves and racks at different heights. Choose an adjustable system so you can rearrange it easily as your storage needs change.

BASEMENT BASICS

Many specialty storage stores will design closets for you at no charge. Simply bring in a sketch of the available space with dimensions and a list of items you want to store. You'll explore design ideas as well as suggestions for specialty storage features. You also can design closets at online stores or purchase professional design ideas.

Under-Stair Storage Ideas

Right: Space beneath these stairs becomes a home office with the addition of a built-in desk and storage drawers.

An often-overlooked spot for storage is the area beneath the staircase. This wedge of space can be walled off with a door for access and serve as an ordinary closet. Or think creatively. Consider the possibilities shown here.

Above: If your stairwell is adjacent to the basement living area, transform the space underneath into shelves for home electronics. Install a pullout shelf for convenient TV watching. Build shelves into every nook and cranny to store CDs, DVDs, tapes, and games.

Right: Built-in shelves, tucked neatly under a staircase, offer the beginnings of a cozy reading nook. Complete the corner with a comfy chair and ottoman, and don't forget good lighting.

Left: Display cubbies and cabinets follow the line of this staircase to create a dramatic focal point. To showcase collections, add lighting inside the niches.
Below: Mullioned glass-pane doors make this smart under-stair hideaway look as if it's always been there. Baskets placed on the shelves become stylish, functional storage compartments within the space.

Create a Floor Plan

These two floor plans model creativity with a few angles in basic spaces. In the plan on the left, for example, the kitchen peninsula angles out from the sink wall for added interest. In the plan on the right, an ordinary hallway gains style on the diagonal.

To determine how you want to use your basement space, create a basic floor plan, such as those shown here. Start by doing a scale drawing of the existing basement layout using a photocopy of the grid paper on page 65. One square equals one foot of floor space. Draw the footprint, or perimeter outline, of the basement as seen from above, and include details such as placement of stairs, windows, and heating and cooling equipment, as well as notations regarding problems, such as a planned bedroom with an existing window that doesn't

meet egress code requirements. Use the architectural symbols, *opposite below,* to indicate these features.

Occasionally posts, ducts, pipes, and other obstacles complicate basement plans. Carefully map the location of obstructions on the plan view, using dotted lines on the floor plan, and take them into account while planning. Moving a partition wall a couple of feet, for example, may allow you to incorporate a structural post within the wall, effectively camouflaging the pole. Locating a half bath next to a furnace may allow you to

BASEMENT BASICS

There are a number of other planning options besides laying out your floor plan on grid paper. Many home centers offer free planning services, for example. You also can purchase floor planning materials in a kit. Or consider computer software specially designed to let you experiment with a variety of layout schemes.

When considering floor-plan options for your finished basement, think about elevations (the vertical wall space). Consider including such attractive and practical features as these built-in display niches and shelves. Faux suede panels provide a handsome backdrop for artwork and collections.

build a single partition wall that encloses the bathroom and also creates a service closet that hides the mechanical equipment.

In addition to a floor plan, you also may want to create scale views of the basement interior walls from the side to indicate potential problems and to illustrate proposed solutions. A side view is also ideal for planning more complex storage systems consisting of shelves, bins, cubbies, drawers, and other features.

If your plans include exterior alterations, you may want to draw exterior views too. Making a scale drawing that incorporates all the proposed changes will give you a good idea of what your house will look like when the project is finished.

MAKING ARRANGEMENTS

Here are some suggestions for arranging rooms and furnishings.

- **Direct traffic.** If traffic passes through a room, it doesn't have to run through the center. Think of your furnishings as walls or guideposts that can funnel traffic.
- **Float furnishings.** Pull pieces away from walls into close-knit groupings with major seating no more than 8 feet apart.
- **Keep convenience within reach.** Include a handy resting place—end tables, stack of books, or short cabinets—for drinks or books near every seat.
- **Maximize a small room.** Use a large-scale piece, such as an armoire or a substantial sofa or loveseat, to anchor the room and create grandeur. Use vertical storage in tight spaces.
- **Fix low ceilings.** "Raise" a low ceiling by drawing the eye upward with floor-to-ceiling window treatments and tall furniture, such as an armoire. Direct traffic away from any low-hanging ceiling obstructions.

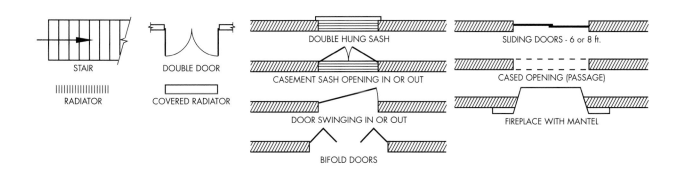

STAIR

DOUBLE DOOR

RADIATOR

COVERED RADIATOR

DOUBLE HUNG SASH

CASEMENT SASH OPENING IN OR OUT

DOOR SWINGING IN OR OUT

BIFOLD DOORS

SLIDING DOORS - 6 or 8 ft.

CASED OPENING (PASSAGE)

FIREPLACE WITH MANTEL

Create a Floor Plan

Use a photocopier to reproduce these templates at 100 percent. Set the copies atop a protected surface, and use a crafts knife to precisely cut out the images. (For sturdier templates, glue the backs of the copies to thin cardboard.) Using the grid on page 65 (or a series of photocopied grids taped together), manipulate the templates to experiment with arrangements.

Dining tables and chairs

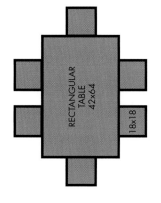

Bathroom fixtures and exercise equipment

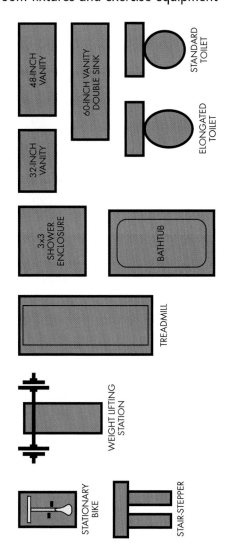

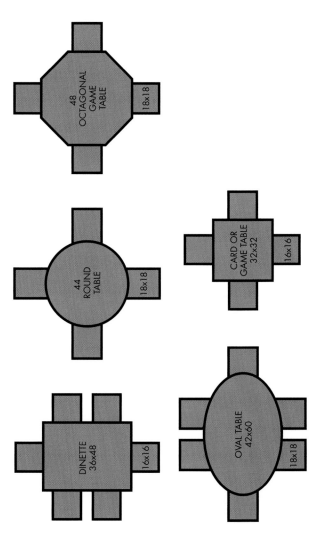

Occasional tables and special pieces

Seating and storage

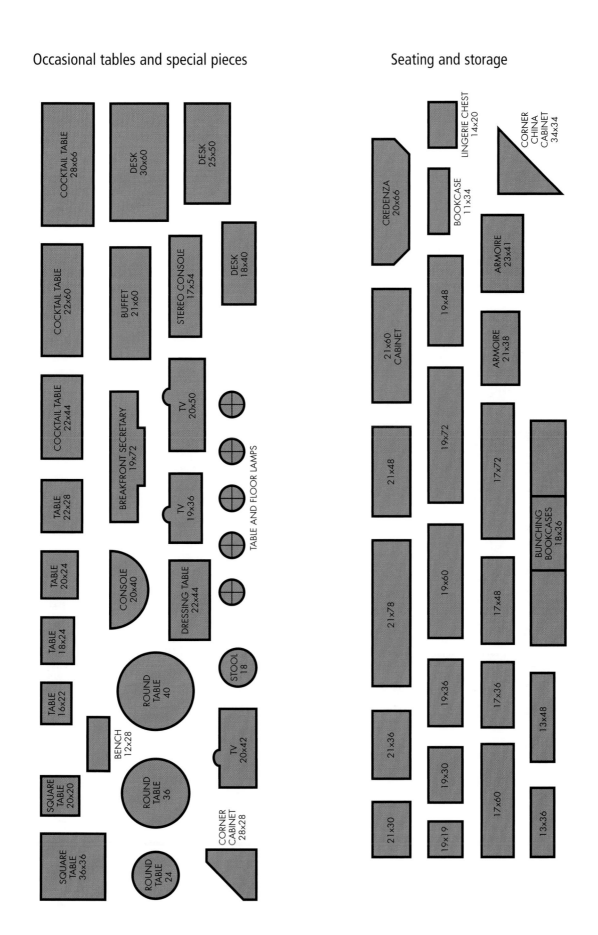

COCKTAIL TABLE
28x66

DESK
30x60

DESK
25x50

COCKTAIL TABLE
22x60

BUFFET
21x60

STEREO CONSOLE
17x54

DESK
18x40

COCKTAIL TABLE
22x44

BREAKFRONT SECRETARY
19x72

TV
20x50

TABLE
22x28

TV
19x36

TABLE AND FLOOR LAMPS

TABLE
20x24

CONSOLE
20x40

DRESSING TABLE
22x44

TABLE
18x24

TABLE
16x22

ROUND TABLE
40

STOOL
18

BENCH
12x28

SQUARE TABLE
20x20

ROUND TABLE
36

TV
20x42

SQUARE TABLE
36x36

ROUND TABLE
24

CORNER CABINET
28x28

LINGERIE CHEST
14x20

CORNER CHINA CABINET
34x34

CREDENZA
20x66

BOOKCASE
11x34

ARMOIRE
23x41

19x48

21x60 CABINET

ARMOIRE
21x38

19x72

21x48

17x72

19x60

17x48

BUNCHING BOOKCASES
18x36

21x78

19x36

17x36

13x48

21x36

19x30

17x60

13x36

21x30

19x19

Create a Floor Plan

An arrangement such as the one in this lower-level family room encourages conversation without stealing attention from the fireplace.

Use a photocopier to reproduce this grid at its original size. To plan large spaces, make more than one copy and tape the grids together. Copy and cut out the templates on pages 62–63 to experiment with floor plans. Note that on the grid, each square is equal to 1 foot.

As you create your plan on grid paper, you also might find these tools handy: tracing paper for alternative overlays, a ruler or straightedge to help keep lines straight, sticky notes for jotting down ideas, and assorted colored pencils to more clearly differentiate features in the space.

BASEMENT BASICS

A sharp pencil and a good ruler will help you draw out the footprint of your available basement space on copies of the grid paper, *opposite*. Take the opportunity to dream a little and experiment with creative alternatives to traditional square rooms. Consider paying an architect or an architectural designer an hourly fee to review your ideas and offer suggestions.

Room
by Room

Well-planned details make every room in the basement as functional and comfortable as possible. These guidelines and tips point the way.

Every room you're planning for your basement serves a particular purpose. To ensure that each one ultimately meets—and even exceeds—those expectations, this chapter features the important details for some of the most desirable spaces. Though lighting is often an afterthought, you'll find it first in this section because most basements lack natural light, making fixture choices even more critical. Put lighting on your list of priorities for each room to make your finished basement as appealing at night as it is during the day. Also don't hesitate to consult with a lighting professional—such as an interior designer or lighting dealer—to obtain advice on choosing types of fixtures and where to wisely locate them in your plan. Then study the specific tips for planning the rooms you want to create, including a home theater, family room, bedroom and bath, kitchen and wet bar (along with tips for including Universal Design principles in your rooms, see pages 80), and a space for your hobbies.

Lighting

Bringing your basement out of the dark begins with an effective lighting plan. Ask the staff at a lighting store or home center to help you plan a lighting scheme that meets your needs. Knowing some lighting basics will help you make your visit more productive.

Almost any room can benefit from at least two layers of illumination: general and task lighting. You should also consider a third layer: accent lighting.

General, or ambient, lighting creates a uniform overall glow in a space using one central ceiling fixture or a series of fixtures. If you prefer, larger floor lamps and torchères can also provide ambient lighting.

Backing up the general lighting plan is the task-lighting layer. These are targeted fixtures that eliminate shadows and shed light directly onto areas where you work (such as a countertop in the laundry room), where you play (such as a pool table), and where you plan to read.

As you might guess, accent (or mood) lighting occurs when you aim light on an object or surface simply to show it off. For

BASEMENT BASICS

When accenting framed artwork, you can avoid glare on the glass by positioning the ceiling fixture far enough out from the wall so the fixture is tilted at a 30-degree angle and the light beam falls on the center of the artwork. Letting light strike an object from one or two sides enhances the dimensional look, while placing the beam straight in front of the object makes it appear flat.

this job you need a lightbulb with a beam that's three to five times brighter than the general lighting.

Recessed cans offer an excellent means for creating overall illumination, task lighting, and accent lighting. The unobtrusive design allows them to work well in most any room and with any decorating style. Recessed cans are available in downlight, accent, and "wall washing" models. Group

Moldings in the bar area of this remodeled basement disguise strings of small lights, which are ideal for setting a mood while creating the illusion of a higher ceiling.

downlights for general lighting or direct them onto specific areas.

When choosing recessed fixtures for general lighting needs, use open cans without diffusers. You can use a wall-washer recessed can to highlight interesting wall textures, or aim the adjustable lens of an accent light to spotlight artwork (see "Basement Basics," *opposite*).

Track lights are another versatile fixture option. Because fixtures on the track swivel and shift, you can use this form of lighting for general, task, and accenting purposes. Now available in stylish models—such as fixtures on stretched wire tracks—track lights are a particularly good choice for rooms where you will want to change the scheme function; new track light fixtures

can be added as the need arises. Be careful not to place track light fixtures or any other dropped fixture in a location that interrupts the swing of a cabinet door or a passage door.

Another consideration in your lighting plan is how you'll control the fixtures. It's a good idea to put each layer of lighting on a separate switch so you can control fixtures individually and selectively turn on and off general, task, or mood lighting fixtures.

For even more lighting options, place fixtures on dimmer controls, which allow you to easily raise and lower the light level. For example, bright lighting is desirable when you're cleaning or working, but when you're ready to relax, a lower light level sets a softer mood.

Recessed cans offer good ambient lighting for this basement sitting area. Smaller downlights illuminate objects within the display niches. An adjustable spotlight draws attention to artwork displayed above the fireplace mantel.

Media-Wise Moves

A home theater can be as simple as this big-screen television artfully integrated into one corner of this lower-level recreation room. The fireplace and well-placed seating arrangement make this a cozy spot.

When you're planning a state-of-the-art home theater with sur-roundsound and the works, consult a professional. (Look in your phone directory under "Home Theater" or "Audio/Video.") These guidelines will help you with preliminary plans:

■ Relate screen size to seating distance. For optimum viewing, professional home the-ater installers recommend a seating distance that's 2 to 2½ times the width of a screen. For example, place sofa and chairs 54 to 68 inches from a 27-inch screen.

■ Front-projection systems replicate the feel of a movie theater but require complete darkness. Rear-projection systems and pic-ture tube TVs produce a picture that looks good with lights on or off—critical if you're going to party while you watch.

■ Create full surroundsound with five speakers. Place one speaker on each side of the TV screen, level with your ears when seated, and about 3 feet away from sidewalls.

Place two speakers behind the sofa about 6 to 8 feet off the floor and at least as far apart as the front pair. Put the fifth one on top of the TV to direct the dialogue. Action-movie buffs enjoy a sub-woofer that intensifies the bass as well as those dramatic booms and bangs. Position it beneath the screen.

■ Stash equipment in a ventilated cabinet or shelves so components don't overheat; be careful not to block the vents on the equipment. For easy access to the backs of all the audiovisual components, construct the shelving or cabinet units 4 or 5 feet in front of the basement wall to create a narrow "hallway" behind the units.

■ Choose dimmer light switches instead of the toggle style for optimum light control.

BASEMENT BASICS

With today's fabulous flat panel television screens and surroundsound, creating a theater-like environment is even more feasible. To enhance the setting, consider building stepped platforms to organize seating stadium-style. For best results, do this in a basement with a 9- or 10-foot-high ceiling, although an 8-foot-high ceiling will also work. Build the platforms with sturdy framing of 4×4s and 2×4s to hold the weight of the furniture and people. Then sheath with ½-inch plywood. Finish the platforms with flooring to match the rest of the room.

This elaborate home theater features handsome leather seating and three televisions. The nicely equipped space lies adjacent to a wet bar and a billiards room so the entertainment options are greatly expanded.

Gather and Play

A lower-level family room can serve many functions—from gathering and relaxing with family and friends to playing board games, reading books, or shooting pool. Plan this space well, and it can be part fun zone, part entertaining space, and part home theater. Playing all these roles means this room may be packed full of elements that can conflict with one another. You can achieve harmony in the family room by balancing these zones.

The major built-in focal point in many family rooms is a fireplace. It usually dominates one wall and often dictates the arrangement of everything else in the room. Furniture is usually positioned to take in views of the hearth, though few people spend a lot of time just sitting and watching the flickering flames.

However, if you sit and watch anything, it's probably the television, which creates another prominent point in the room. The TV is often an afterthought, stuck to one side of the fireplace because that is where it can be seen. Unfortunately, in this scenario, neither the fireplace nor the television gets attention. When two elements compete for focus, the best solution may be to give each equal treatment, positioning the firebox and television screen at the same height and using similar cabinet or wall treatments around both elements, such as in the family room, *opposite below*.

A family room also needs to be designed for more than watching TV or enjoying a crackling fire. Most people want bookshelves, comfortable conversation areas, and an area or table for playing games. Built-ins and multipurpose furniture can create these spaces without overcrowding a room or consuming floor space that may be needed to entertain. Use task lighting to help define individual activity areas and to allow adequate visibility without overlighting the rest of the room.

FIT IN A POOL TABLE

If you want to include a pool table, *left*, in your family room plans, keep these recommended clearances for comfortable play in mind:

• For a 7-foot, bar-size pool table equipped with 48-inch-long cues, your room can be as small as 11×13½ feet. For 52-inch-long cues, the room should measure 11½×14 feet. When using 57-inch-long cues on a 7-foot table, the room should be at least 12½×15 feet.

• A standard 8-foot table will work in a 12×15½-foot room if you use 48-inch-long cues. If you increase cue length to 52 inches, plan a room at least 12½×16 feet. For cues measuring 57 inches long, the room should measure a minimum of 13½×17 feet.

• If you're truly serious about pool, you may prefer a 9-foot tournament-size pool table. This size, coupled with 57-inch-long cues, requires a room measuring at least 14×18 feet.

• For lighting, the bottom of the fixture shade should hang 31 inches above the playing surface.

Kid smarts

When creating a special area for children's play, keep these suggestions in mind:

■ **Safety.** Make sure the play area features an egress window or other exit.

■ **Materials.** Choose durable, easy-to-clean wall and floor treatments.

■ **Fun.** Mount a big mirror securely on the wall; children love to play in front of them. (Keep it away from the scooters, though.) Paint one wall with chalkboard paint so the kids can write and draw on the wall with chalk. Or install an erasable marker board.

■ **Cleanup.** Kids will be more likely to pick up their toys if you provide see-through storage solutions. Shelves, stacking bins, and hooks make finding a child's favorite things and remembering what goes where easier.

■ **Inspire.** Stimulate play with high-contrast color schemes. Black-and-white and vibrant, opposing colors are energizing.

Paint and durable carpet transformed this basement corner into a child's play haven. On the walls, colorful tackboards give young imaginations full rein for learning and fun.

In this lower-level family room, a cozy seating area makes best use of the fireplace and the television—which are positioned on adjacent walls with simple surrounds of drywall and wood trim.

Home Office

If you work full time out of your home or frequently require a home office, you'll appreciate the privacy and quiet that a basement office can offer. Primary requirements for an office are light, heat, and sufficient wiring to handle telephone lines, computers, fax machines, and printers. You also need cable or wiring to connect the computer to your Internet service provider (ISP).

Adding stud walls provides the space to run new wiring. Because existing wiring is usually exposed in the overhead joists, it's easy to extend an electrical circuit or add a telephone jack. Adding a separate circuit to serve just your computer and other office equipment prevents drawing too much power from a single circuit that can trip circuit breakers and cause the loss of unsaved work. Consult a licensed electrician about adding a new circuit. Allow enough electrical outlets so you can move equipment

around, add equipment later, or change the layout of your office.

Proper lighting is especially important to anyone spending long hours working in an office. Remember to provide both ambient and task lighting.

If your basement is especially humid, be sure to install a portable dehumidifier to protect books, documents, and sensitive electronics. You'll also want to include plenty of shelves, drawers, and an other storage for supplies, papers, books, and magazines. In addition to a desk with open work surface, consider a separate table and chairs in one corner of the office to provide an additional surface for papers and to serve as a conference area.

Locating your home office near the basement wet bar can provide a convenient location for making coffee as well as offer access to the refrigerator for soft drinks and snacks.

Right: No pipes, ductwork, or stairs were moved to create this home office. Built around an exterior wall used for storage, the shelving/desk unit provides room for two to work or meet with clients. **Below:** The standard basement window shown here is barely recognizable because it's worked into the storage wall and set off with eggplant-color paint. The glass entry door at one end of the office provides a safe stairwell exit.

BASEMENT BASICS

Make your home office as comfortable and organized as possible. After all, you may spend a lot of hours at work (even if it is at home). Treat yourself to a palette of your favorite colors and include amenities that can ease tasks, such as a copier and a conference table. Include plenty of storage space for files and supplies. Your office can also pull double duty with a sofa sleeper for overnight guests.

A staircase with an open banister keeps the petite study from feeling cramped. Recessed cans provide general lighting, while recessed spots handle task lighting over the desk—there are no foreboding areas in this basement. A mix of textures—stained wood, painted woodwork, nubby carpet, and denim upholstery—creates a fresh, clean, comfortable look.

Bedrooms

Naturally cool and quiet, a basement bedroom can become one of the most inviting retreats in the house. As you plan, consider the best dimensions for your needs. A good size for a bedroom is a minimum of 125 square feet to comfortably fit a double bed and 150 square feet for two twin beds.

Codes usually require a wall-mounted light switch immediately inside the door. You also must provide direct access to the outside—an egress—in case of fire or other emergency. If your basement is not a walk-out, plan for an egress window or door. (See more about egress exits on page 39.)

Be sure to install a smoke alarm outside the bedroom door and another over the stairway. A carbon monoxide alarm is also an important addition.

In the bedroom, carpeting provides warmth and comfort underfoot. In the ceiling, fiberglass insulation between joists quiets the sound of footsteps overhead. Consider shrubbery or a fence in front of windows to enhance privacy.

Locate a bathroom near—or even adjoining—the bedroom as an added convenience for overnight guests. Be sure to include storage for linens as well as for any toiletries, cleaning products, and other necessities.

If you're short on space in the basement, consider furnishing the bedroom to serve multiple functions. For example, include an armoire that opens to reveal a home office. Or furnish the space as a home office and install a pull-down Murphy bed in one wall so the room can also serve as a guest room.

Opposite: **Located in a walk-out basement, this bedroom features three twin beds to accommodate overnight guests. The patio door satisfies egress requirements as it makes the room more bright and gives visitors access to a private patio.**

Right: **In this lower-level bedroom, placing the bed on the diagonal cultivates the illusion of a larger space and makes room for small areas of interest, such as the sitting spot beside the patio door. The small area rug, placed on the same angle as the bed, emphasizes the diagonal. A trunk at the foot of the bed plays up the bed as a focal point.**

BE YOUR GUEST

Ever wonder if your guests are really comfortable in the extra bedroom? The best way to find out is to spend the night in the room yourself—you'll quickly learn what's missing. To make overnight visitors feel more at home, include some of the following special touches in the guest room and nearby bathroom: Keep a pitcher of fresh water and glasses beside the bed. Stack a few good books and magazines. If there's enough space, add a television and a writing desk with stationery and pens. Be sure the bathroom has plenty of fluffy towels and basic toiletries, such as you find in better hotels.

Bathrooms

Including a bathroom in your basement finishing plans is sure to increase the value of your home and promises convenience for you, your family, and guests.

Adding a bathroom to the basement isn't much different from fitting one in on the main level; the closer you can locate the bathroom to the main drain line, however, the easier the installation for a shower and toilet.

The job may require cutting and removing concrete to splice into the existing drain line. One solution is to elevate the new bathroom—if you have the headroom available—to create underfoot space in which to conceal new plumbing lines and a drain.

If you are building a new house and are considering an additional bathroom in the basement for sometime in the future, be sure your builder understands your plans and roughs in the necessary plumbing at the proper locations. It's much easier and much less expensive to provide for your future plumbing needs now than to add them after concrete floors are poured and the foundation walls are constructed.

Mirrors stretch wall to wall and countertop to ceiling to make this modest 5×7-foot basement bathroom seem bigger than it is. The mirror also increases light by creating the illusion of "double" the windows and recirculating illumination from light fixtures. Checkerboard pattern wallpaper enhances perspective in the reflection. A space-saving sink that measures 18 inches, front to back, saves on valuable counter space too.

Matching ceramic tiles covering the walls and floor in this bathroom make the space look bigger. Solid color and lack of pattern are the secrets. An angled shower to the right uses the space more efficiently.

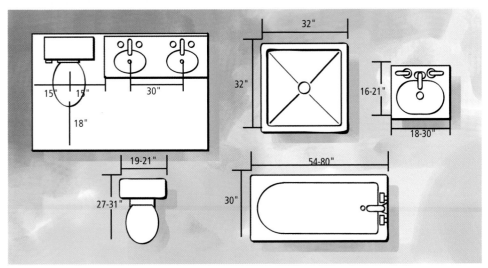

These illustrations show how much space is needed for both bath fixtures as well as the clearance to use them comfortably. If you have an odd-shape space, you probably can find a fixture to fit it.

A kitchen in the basement can be as large and well-equipped as a main-level kitchen. Designed as an L-shape with an island, this plan features a peninsula that easily doubles as a snack bar or as a serving buffet during parties.

Kitchens and Universal Design

Your basement may be able to accommodate a fully equipped, full-size kitchen or a mini-kitchen with fewer amenities and less space requirements—the choice depends on your needs and available space.

If you have live-in relatives or a nanny, you may want to consider a complete kitchen with full-size appliances and upper and lower cabinetry. For most people, a wet bar or kitchenette will serve low-key daily needs as well as high-end parties.

To create a wet bar or kitchenette, you'll need access to hot and cold water for a bar sink as well as electrical outlets for an under-counter refrigerator, a microwave oven, small countertop appliances, and possibly a small dishwasher or dishwasher drawer. You'll also need to choose cabinetry and countertop materials. For wine storage, consider a small wine refrigerator or wine racks.

When designing a wet bar, the countertop and cabinetry can be arranged to separate the bar area from the adjoining room. Or recess a short length of cabinetry and countertop into the family-room wall and provide pocket doors to close off the bar when not in use.

Proving that Universal Design can be as beautiful as it is practical, this stunning marble-lined bath features a shower without doors or a raised threshold, making it easily accessible. The low sink offers room for someone in a wheelchair to maneuver more closely to the countertop.

UNIVERSAL DESIGN

You may be familiar with Universal Design as a set of architectural concepts that make a home more livable for the handicapped or elderly. Universal Design is about flexibility and easy access—making them good standards not only for the kitchen and bathroom, but for any room in the house. Incorporating Universal Design aspects into your basement project creates a more comfortable space and makes using the space easier for anyone suffering from a bad back, using crutches or a wheelchair, or healing from a broken arm or leg. A handful of Universal Design concepts follows. To carry the concept further, search your library or the Internet for Universal or Accessible Home Design. One organization worth noting is The Center for Universal Design at the North Carolina State University School of Design (www.design.ncsu.edu/cud/).

• Become familiar with the comfortable reach range. Put door handles, appliances, electrical switches, and outlets 15 to 48 inches above the floor so everyone will be able to reach them comfortably.

• Fit cupboards and cabinets with rollout drawers so contents can be pulled into view.

• Choose refrigerator drawers over traditional stand-up models.

• Craft threshold-free, step-free entries, and plan bump-free transitions between flooring materials.

• Make sink counters no taller than 34 inches; allow knee clearances of 27 inches high, 30 inches wide, and 19 inches deep. Choose lever or wrist-blade-style faucets and scald-proof, thermostatically controlled valves.

• Allow 4-foot passageways from one space to the next.

• Allow 5-foot approach room near beds and activity areas. This allows room for wheelchairs room to turn around.

• In baths, arrange curb-free shower rooms with handheld, height-adjustable showerheads. Frame the walls with blocking so you can install grab bars where needed. (See page 78 for more on planning baths.)

This laundry center tucks out of sight behind a pair of bifold doors. The movable center island in the foreground is ideal for folding laundry.

Laundry Room

Plenty of cabinetry for storing detergent, dryer sheets, stain remover, and other laundry supplies helps keep this laundry room organized. A separate closet is sized especially for laundry baskets, which are handy for sorting dirty laundry or for storing clean laundry when ready for folding.

One of the benefits of a basement laundry room is keeping the inevitable tangle of clothes and noise from disrupting the rest of the house. Make your lower-level laundry room more efficient with moisture-proof surfaces, plenty of storage, bins for sorting laundry, and surfaces for folding. An ironing board that folds down out of the wall adds convenience and saves storage space. A television lets you keep up with the news as you work.

Typical laundry hookups include hot and cold water supply lines and a drainage system—items readily accessible in a basement. Gas dryers need access to gas lines. Both electric and gas dryers need venting to the outside. Also add a floor drain to handle spills or overflows from a malfunctioning washing machine.

Other additions to your basement laundry room worth considering include a deep-basin sink or combination shower/basin, a sewing center, an area for doing crafts projects or potting flowers, and a laundry chute that connects to upstairs bedrooms as well as the kitchen.

Paneled closet doors near the bathroom keep a stacked washer and dryer out of sight when not in use.

MAKE AN OPEN-AND-SHUT CASE FOR LAUNDRY

If your transformed basement displaces a sprawling, baskets-everywhere laundry room, resolve the issue with an organized laundry-in-a-closet like this one. You need a 6×3-foot slice of space—less for a stacked washer and dryer. Fit the closet with a 4-foot fluorescent lighting fixture and a shelf to hold detergent and other laundry necessities. You also need:

• Access to utilities: hot and cold water supply lines, a drainage system, and electrical outlets.
• An exterior wall location so the dryer can be vented to the outdoors.
• A floor drain to handle overflows or leaks. To achieve the required amount of downslope for your drainpipe, you may need to place the appliances on a platform. Consult a plumbing professional or your local building code official for assistance.

As an alternative, locate a stacked washer and dryer on one side of the closet with shelves and space to hang clothes to dry.

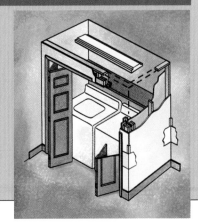

Individual adhesive-back carpet squares—flooring easily installed by novice do-it-yourselfers—add comfort underfoot in this modest exercise room. If one of the squares becomes stained, it's easy to remove and replace.

Exercise and More

If you've ever allowed a treadmill to languish in an out-of-the-way corner of the house, consider creating a special space in your basement designed especially for exercise. A well-designed exercise room, outfitted with quality equipment, is more likely to be used regularly. Converting basement space into an exercise room is relatively easy because little, if any, plumbing or electrical work is required.

Create a workout environment suited to your style, whether it's quiet and meditative or energizing with sights and sounds. If you're adding 2×4 walls, remember to run the wires and cable for stereo and television before covering the studs with drywall. Fixing a television to a swiveling, ceiling-mounted bracket or creating a built-in niche in the wall allows you to view the set from anywhere in the room. Include a VCR or DVD player to view exercise videos.

Install tough, durable flooring—vinyl, rubber, or cork tiles are appropriate choices. Evaluate your workout techniques with mirror panels covering the walls. Plan the space on paper first, and provide a minimum of 30 inches of space between exercise equipment. (Use the graph paper on page 65.)

Simple saunas

Imagine slipping into your very own hot sauna after a tough day at work. You can! Many Scandinavian families enjoy their saunas every day. Such luxury—and all the health benefits that go with it—is a surprisingly simple project. So think about including one in your finished basement plans. All you need is a 3×4-foot space, structural walls to frame the shell, and electric hookups. Prepackaged sauna kits include all the equipment, controls, and interior finish materials you need. Saunas use dry heat and require 110-volt household current; there's no need for a separate circuit or plumbing and drains. Search the Internet for sauna kits; you'll find several companies that offer them in sizes ranging from 3×4 to 12×12 feet at prices that vary widely.

The most affordable kits have walls that are lined with hemlock, spruce, and fir, and have fewer, more modest features such as light fixtures, backrests, towel bars, and timing controls. More expensive kits have cedar or redwood walls and finer amenities.

Any type of sauna is sure to relax you. Almost as relaxing is knowing that installing one won't throw your back or your budget out of whack.

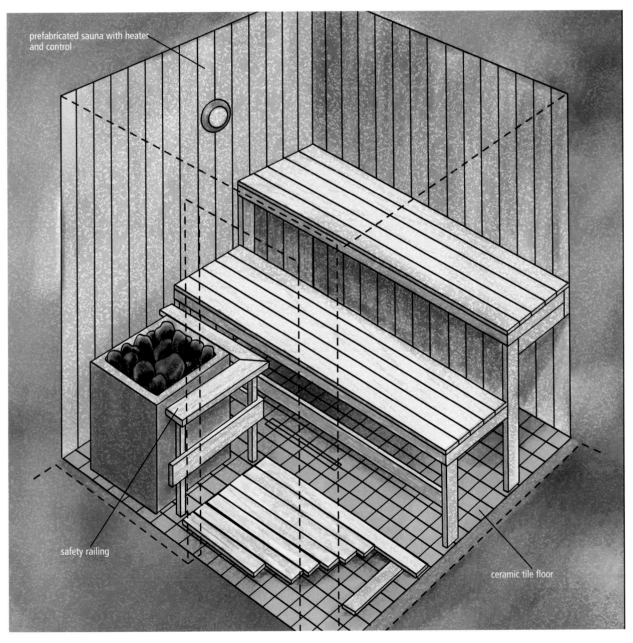

prefabricated sauna with heater and control

safety railing

ceramic tile floor

Wine Connoisseurs

Below: An undercounter wine refrigerator coupled with a long countertop becomes an ideal serving buffet for parties.

Bottom right: The customized storage next to the wine cooler keeps glassware organized and close.

You may want to dedicate an entire room to storing wine or just have a refrigerator especially designed for displaying and cooling the bottles. Either way, the basement is just the place to bring your dream wine collection to life with spectacular results.

You can build and insulate a room from scratch, or check with a number of companies that offer kits for creating a cooled, walk-in room. To keep the conditioned air in and warm air out, install 2×4 walls with rigid foam insulation and vapor barriers on both sides. The door should be insulated and weather-sealed. Refrigerator-type wine cooling units in a variety of sizes and styles are also available.

Here are some suggestions for creating your own basement wine cellar:

■ **Cool and dry.** Wines last longer when stored at temperatures between 50°F and 58°F. To keep white wine cooler than red, store these bottles on the bottom racks and the red on top because cold air naturally settles at floor level. If your basement is humid, be sure to keep humidity levels low with a dehumidifier.

■ **Rack 'em up.** Most wine bottles should be stored on their sides in racks—purchased or custom-made—so the cork won't dry out. A dry cork shrinks and the bottle will no longer be properly sealed. Make sure the racks are good quality and strong enough to hold the weight of the bottles, which can weigh up to 3 pounds each.

■ **Stay organized.** Store bottles on racks according to the types of wines to make it easy to find the one you want.

■ **Have a seat.** Complete your room with a table and chairs or with a bar area and stools so you and your guests can snack and chat while you taste the wine.

Above: Furnish your wine room like any other gathering space in the house to make it as inviting as possible. This elegant wine room, for example, boasts handsome artwork, pendant lighting, and comfortable seating.
Left: An 18th-century French sideboard and floor-to-ceiling racks provide plenty of storage in this wine room. Wall racks, such as these, should be secured to studs to support the weight of the bottles.

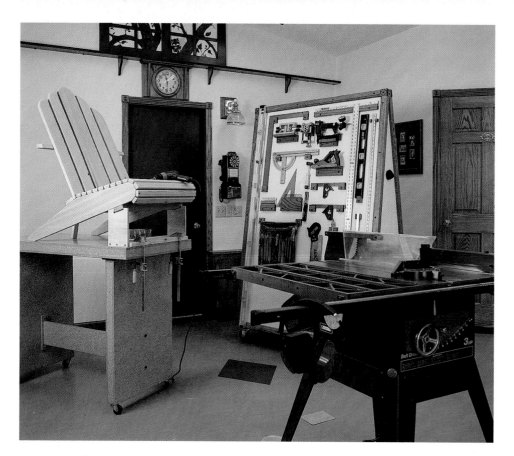

Workbenches and large power tools on rollers offer a flexible arrangement for this nicely equipped workshop. The A-frame rack can be rolled anywhere in the room so the tools it holds are always within reach.

Special Interests

Grown-ups need places for play too. Devoting basement space to your hobbies makes your favorite pastime even more enjoyable.

Start by estimating how much space your hobby requires. Some hobby spaces call for a specialized shape or more square footage than others. Feeding an 8-foot board through woodworking machinery may call for a work space at least 16 feet long—much larger than a quilting studio might require, for example.

Working with awkwardly shaped materials, such as sheets of plywood, may require a workspace with ceilings higher than the conventional 8 feet. Modeling, electronics, or other hobbies may require only a desk-size space.

One advantage of a dedicated hobby room over a dual-purpose space is the ability to add customized conveniences. Install a utility sink for worry-free cleanup or a ready water source. Wire in 220-volt outlets and electrical breakers to accommodate commercial-quality tools.

Some hobbies are noisier and messier than others, so consider how your hobby space will relate to the rest of the house. Additional soundproofing and solid-core doors for a music room, for example, will help keep practice sessions muted from the rest of the household.

Think about lighting needs too. If you enjoy painting or drawing, you may want illumination that mimics natural light, such as halogen task lighting. By contrast, a woodworking shop benefits from an abundance of bright, fluorescent light fixtures.

A hobby room's decor also can be influenced by your hobby, so install display spaces to show off your projects. After all, a hobby room should not only allow for accomplishments, it should inspire them.

BOOST YOUR CREATIVITY

• Prevent muscle fatigue that comes from standing on hard surfaces by placing soft, nonslip rubber mats where you'll be working (available at restaurant supply outlets). If you don't like the look, toss decorative rugs over them.
• Dedicate electrical circuits to individual pieces of equipment. Route the circuits through a subpanel with a master switch that allows you to turn off the power to all equipment when the shop is not in use.
• Soundproof your workshop if your work is noisy (or if your work requires peace and quiet). Install a fan and at least two operable windows for ventilation and to direct exhaust fumes out of the house.

A family of crafters revels in this workshop. They can see what's available to work with at a glance, thanks to a wall of white modular shelving units and many see-through boxes, bins, and letter trays that organize colorful supplies and tools. The laminate easy-to-clean table provides enough room for everyone to gather.

A walk-out basement with easy access to the backyard is an ideal location for potting. This one features an antique dry sink for old-fashioned flavor and a metal lining in the top for filling pots with soil and watering flowers. A nearby sink aids cleanup, and plenty of open shelving keeps supplies at the ready.

Beautify Your Basement

You're about to embark on one of the most rewarding steps in the finishing process—breathing your own character and style into your new lower-level rooms.

Opposite: Even without the glorious water view, your basement living spaces can be as refreshing and beautiful as this lower-level bedroom. Smart choices in colors, textures, fabrics, paints, and other elements make it happen.

Decorating a basement calls for many of the same strategies and materials that work well for upper-level living spaces. Color, for example, makes any room more inviting and livable. Take this time to look into the art and science of color usage, take a look at some of the ways you can spruce up rooms with texture, fabric, and paints. The ideas for moldings will help you dress up a basic, boxy room. You'll also find creative approaches for floors and ceilings and clever treatments for basement windows. Of course, your rooms aren't complete without deftly arranged furnishings and artwork as well as some space-saving and efficient built-in storage. After you've brought all these elements together into an eye-appealing package, you'll begin to appreciate your accomplishment: gaining valuable living space for much less than building an addition or moving into a new home.

Coloring Lessons

Color can make your basement as bright and beautiful as upper-level rooms, allowing you to make the spaces sizzle, soothe, or charm—the choice is yours to make. Knowing the science behind the hues you love can help you fold color into your decorating plans without fear of creating clashes.

Hold a prism up to the light and you'll cast a rainbow around the room simply by shifting the position of the prism. This mini-science experiment is also your first lesson in choosing color for your basement. When white light shines through a prism, it separates the light into the spectrum of colors, each with its own wavelength. Color is the reflection of light on an object created by waves of a certain length, say those of blue, absorbing the rest. The color red has the longest wavelength and violet the shortest.

Color relationships

The progression of color from longest to shortest wavelengths is traditionally presented on a color wheel of 12 hues. Colors opposite each other on the wheel are called "complementary" colors. For a striking and energizing scheme, combine complementary colors—red with green, purple with yellow, orange with blue—because these hues play off each other with the most contrast. If you prefer a decor with less contrast, one using "analogous" colors—those adjacent to each other on the color wheel—may give you the desired effect. "Monochromatic" color schemes incorporate shades and tints of a single hue. A monochromatic blue scheme, for example, might feature navy, royal, and sky. Incorporating variations of a single color can be soothing and sophisticated (cool neutrals) or exciting and vivacious (variations of a hot tropical color).

Warm or cool?

You've probably noticed that you look best in either warm or cool colors. The thinking

---

THE COLOR WHEEL

A color wheel is made of 12 hues: three primary colors, three secondaries, and six tertiaries. Color relationships built on these color groups form the basis of design color theory. Any combination of colors can work beautifully together—beauty being in the eye of the beholder—but understanding the color wheel and some theory makes experimenting with color all the more fun.

PRIMARY. Red, blue, and yellow are the primary hues. These colors are pure—you can't create them from other colors, and all other colors are created from them.

SECONDARY. Orange, green, and violet are secondary hues. They sidle up next to the primaries on the color wheel because they are formed when equal parts of two primary colors are combined.

TERTIARY. Mixing a primary color with the secondary color next to it creates a tertiary color. With each blending—primary with primary, then primary with secondary—the resulting hues become less vivid. Red plus orange, for example, makes an orange-red color; blue plus green makes a green-blue, and so on.

---

behind your cloth color decisions can translate to your home decorating too (although you don't have to paint your walls pink just because it's one of "your colors"). Warm colors—red, orange, yellow—round out one side of the color wheel, while cool colors—blue, green, violet—reside on the other. Blending colors can add visual heat or chill. Green, for instance, can be warmed by adding some yellow—which might take the visual chill out of a bedroom with a north-facing window well, for example. Or if you're choosing a color for a south-facing recreation room in a walk-out basement, you might want to cool down your green paint with a small amount of blue. Think of the skin of a "cool red" plum that carries purple undertones as opposed to a "warm red" you might see in a ripe tomato.

Color also has the remarkable ability to make things appear larger or smaller. Two aspects of color give it this capacity: temperature and brightness. Warm colors (such as red) seem closer or "advance," cool colors (such as blue) appear farther away or "recede." Likewise darker colors advance, and lighter colors recede. Use this knowledge to choose colors for walls, ceilings, and furnishings, and you can visually stretch or shrink elements to your liking. For example, paint an oversized family room tomato red (a warm color) or forest green (a dark color), and it will seem more cozy and embracing. Add some breathing room to a tiny powder room with walls and ceiling of sky blue (a cool color) or pale lavender (a light color).

The sky's the limit in this basement home theater. A string of tiny white lights behind deep blue acrylic panels creates a starlit sky effect. The soffit below the ceiling and drapery panels repeats the deep blue hues, setting a relaxing mood that encourages you to relax.

Touchable Textures

Texture feels wonderful to your fingers and feet, and your eyes will love the depth and warmth that textured fabrics and surfaces bring to basement rooms.

With the right treatment, walls can introduce a new dimension to the basement. These textural effects lend a charming, old-world feel that's an ideal backdrop for antiques and traditional furnishings. To create a look similar to the wall behind the small cabinet, *below left,* mix four handfuls of 2- to 6-inch-long strands of straw into 1 gallon of drywall compound. Use a 6-inch putty knife to apply a thin coat of the mixture to primed walls. If needed, use your fingers to move pieces of straw into more attractive positions.

You also can imprint designs into texture paint, such as on the wall, *below.* Start with a selection of herbs, leaves, shells, and rocks with interesting surfaces. Then apply a thin coat of texture paint over a primed wall. Dip the collected items in water and randomly press them into the still-wet compound. Pull the object away, leaving their imprints behind. After you completely paint the wall, let it dry. Protect and highlight the wall with pigmented glaze. (See pages 98–99 for more tips on working with glazes.)

Below, right: **Nature provides the tactile pleasures evoked by these two walls. Handfuls of straws are used to create the rustic finish,** *below,* **while impressions of herbs, leaves, shells, and rocks lend interest to the wall,** *right.*

Left: Though the palette is neutral, this basement family room isn't boring. Subtly patterned commercial carpet tiles, velvety chairs, a handcarved saddle, and primitive twig artwork show how a variety of decorative elements, from floor to ceiling, can convey beauty through texture.

Below: Furnishings fashioned from natural materials, such as this wicker chair, work well with nubby fabrics to inject rooms with a pleasing array of textures. Use textured fabrics for upholstery on chairs and ottomans, pillow covers, and window treatments.

BASEMENT BASICS

Handmade tiles offer an appealing, undulating surface that adds interest to walls. On floors, stone tiles, such as slate, feature a surface that's also texturally pleasing, comfortable underfoot, and easy to clean.

Fabric Finesse

Warmth, color, texture, softness, pattern—fabrics can bring all these pleasing points of interest into a room.

Soft and textural, fabric offers a gentle alternative to paper when used on the wall, as in this bathroom, *left*. Start by stapling on a layer of acrylic batting for a plush look, then stretch and staple lengths of fabric across the wall. Decorative green-and-tan welting, secured with a glue gun, conceals the staples here. Although the lower portion of the walls appears to be bamboo strips on wood wainscoting, the entire effect is created with paint. Fabric also can be used to finish the ceiling in the basement—simply staple lengths of fabric to joists and hide seams and staples with decorative cording or ribbon. Or allow fabric to gently swag, such as the ceiling treatment in the child's playroom shown on page 9.

Above: Fabric outlined in decorative cording gives these bathroom walls a soft, finished touch.

Right: Generously sprinkle a variety of pillows throughout rooms to promote a sense of comfort and warmth. These pillows infuse the setting with pleasing patterns and playful colors. Decorative embellishments and fringes inject even more style and interest.

An alternative to stretching fabric on walls is to allow it to drape luxuriously. Sheets offer a quick way to employ this technique. They're already hemmed, and many come in coordinating prints. Have fun with your hanging hardware: Use pegs or attach ribbon loops to fabric and hang them over glass doorknobs or colorful, shaped hardware.

MASTER THE MIX

Florals, stripes, and prints may seem like odd companions, but when combined correctly, they can give any room a comfortable, inviting look. The way to mix patterns and prints, however, can seem puzzling at times. Here are some basics that lead to a successful blend.

Use the principles of pattern. While there are no hard-and-fast rules for mixing patterns, keep in mind that too much of a good thing can overwhelm. When you're not sure about what works with a particular pattern, rely on stripes to balance your blend. Like solids, stripes mix with everything.

Stay close to a certain style. A bold contemporary print and a small country print, for example, may not be compatible.

Pay attention to scale. Patterns and prints should also complement the scale of the room or the piece of furniture. Petite designs work well on pillows, dust ruffles, and small windows. Large patterns are better suited to walls, bedspreads, and draperies.

Vary scale within a room. Too many large patterns will compete; too many small prints will lack a focal point. If you feel unsure, try this formula: one large-scale print, one medium stripe, one small dark print, and one small light print.

Find the color link. To help you link two or more patterns, watch for common colors, such as in the photograph, *right*. Various motifs will look like parts of a family when they share even a small amount of a similar hue.

Go with the pros. Flip through magazines and books of wall coverings and patterns to get ideas about what patterns and prints work well together. Many companies offer premixed collections. If you prefer not to go that route, just look for patterns similar to yours, and see how the professionals use the mix.

Watch the swatch. Finally, you fall for several patterns, but will they work together? Bring home samples or large swatches of the fabrics and wallpapers you're considering mixing. Then lay them out in your room. Or better yet, tape them to the wall. Now live with them for a week or so, and see whether they grow on you or quickly wear out their welcome.

Painted Personality

Some people think of paint as a liquid asset. That's because of its unlimited potential for transforming most any surface and making your basement brighter and more beautiful. Experiment with these glazing techniques to create your custom liquid asset.

Glazing liquid is the medium that gives depth to decorative finishes. Milky in appearance, it dries clear, makes paint transparent, is workable, and allows thin layers of color for a deeper, more professional look. The simple applications shown here use latex (water-base) glaze and paints that are easy to work with, dry quickly, and clean up with soap and water.

Before applying glaze to the wall, experiment with the base-coat color and the amount of color you add to the glaze. Glazes also come pre-tinted in a variety of hues—ideal for warming up or cooling down a less-than-perfect base color. A selection of sheens—flat, pearlescent, and more—is also available. Practice a few times with the glaze and application technique you decide to use.

There are two basic ways to apply glaze: a negative application, *below,* and a positive application, *above.* With negative, you apply the colored glaze over the base coat with a paintbrush or sponge brush. Then you remove areas of glaze by rolling or dabbing it away, revealing the base coat. Using a positive application, you dip the tool lightly in the colored glaze, wring it out, and then lightly apply it to the wall.

Right: Applying glaze to a painted wall with a tool is called a positive application. It usually results in lighter colorations and a more subtle pattern.

Below: Removing areas of applied glaze before it dries is called a negative application. It reveals the base coat and often results in stronger colorations and patterns.

BASEMENT BASICS

To enliven existing faux-wood paneling in a basement, lightly sand the surface and wipe with a tack rag. Prime and let dry. Then paint the desired color. As a finishing touch, top with a glaze technique for depth and warmth.

Far left: **Combs** produce straight or curvy lines in negative applications. Comb straight or with a curve from top to bottom on the wall. Or you can comb only below the chair rail where the distance is shorter and lines are easier to control.

Below left: **Mitts** are alternatives to sponging or dabbing. They're one of a variety of tools in crafts stores that help you apply paint and texture easily and evenly.

Left: **Plastic wrap** can be bunched to apply or remove glaze. Or apply larger sheets flat to wet, glazed walls. It adheres and wrinkles on contact. Peel it away to reveal markings that resemble plasterwork.

Below: **Cheesecloth** (far left) can be rolled or dabbed for a fine texture in positive or negative techniques. Wash any cloth before using it to soften and remove lint. **Burlap** (center) offers similar textural results, though more intense. As with cheesecloth, wash before using. **Paper**, *right*, offers a crinkled look with sharp lines when dabbed or rolled. Use large sheets of clean paper, such as brown bags, butcher paper, or blank newsprint.

One option for creating a checkerboard design on a floor is to use a 12-inch tile (or whatever size you prefer) as a template for painting. Lay the tile on the floor, outline the shape in pencil, and slide the tile over to draw the next square. Simple! Use a measuring tape to assure that your lines remain true and parallel.

For a low-cost flooring solution, consider painting the concrete underfoot, such as with a simple checkerboard pattern, *above*. The secret to a long-lasting finish is to use top-of-the-line primer and paint. Use painter's tape to make crisp edges. To finish, top the completed, dry design with several coats of high-quality, nonyellowing clear

BASEMENT BASICS

Quick-release painter's masking tape is the secret behind painting crisp, straight lines on walls and floors. One caveat: If you don't remove the tape before the paint dries, you may pull up some of the paint with the tape.

polyurethane. Lightly sand the second-to-last coat, wipe residue with a tack cloth, and apply the final coat.

Diamonds can be a wall's best friend to lend it dramatic impact. Even a modest-size room, such as this bedroom, *opposite top*, gains a beauty boost from the oversize motif. Paint on the base color first. When dry, snap chalk lines to form the diamonds. (Use colored chalk powder to match the second diamond color.) Tape off the diamonds that will be the second color, and paint. Remove the tape before the paint dries to avoid peeling up paint with the tape. To give the impression of seeing "beyond" some of the wall color and creating the illusion of a larger space, use water to thin the latex paint for the second diamond color. Pale colors make a room seem bigger too.

Create a twist on this traditional harlequin design by using a faux technique and glaze on the alternating diamonds. First decide on a size for the diamonds in the pattern. Then use a measuring tape and a pencil to mark the locations and sizes of the diamonds across the wall. Join the marks and form the outlines of the diamonds by snapping chalk lines. Use quick-release painter's tape to outline alternating diamonds and to achieve crisp edges when applying the thinned latex color.

In this basement play-room, an art gallery theme inspires vibrant hues and a bit of fun. High on the wall, picture molding creates a "window" where art thieves, Gus and Lucky, peer inside. If freehand painting isn't one of your talents, use an opaque projector to shine an image selected from a book or other source onto the wall. Trace the image and—like a coloring book—fill in with paint.

Molding Character

Moldings offer one of the quickest and easiest ways to inject a basic basement with an eye-pleasing dose of architectural interest.

Consider these techniques:

■ Add a chair rail to define a room. Typical heights are 30–36 inches from the floor.

■ To create faux-wall panels, start with picture-frame molding. Mimic wainscoting by painting the spaces between moldings (the "panels") to match the trim. Or use wallpaper insets or contrasting paint for drama.

■ Draw attention to a ceiling by creating one or more frames near the edge. A painted border or even wallpaper can accent a formal design. A trio of closely related painted colors will create subtle interest.

Applications

Whatever design you choose, use these tips to make the work go smoothly:

■ Choose moldings that complement the existing millwork in your house.

■ Mark out your designs with painter's tape first; you'll want to examine proportions and check for level. (Mark guides with a pencil before removing the tape.) Whenever possible, choose painter's tape the same width as your molding.

■ Get samples and experiment with layering molding styles.

■ Using a miter box and handsaw or a compound miter saw, practice miter cuts on wood or molding scraps. Measure to the outside corners, and start the cuts from the thin edges toward the thick side. (If you're not sure about your mitering skills, pay a lumberyard to make your cuts.)

■ Pre-drill the nail holes to avoid splitting the wood.

■ Remember: You can fill and paint over small flaws.

Transform an unassuming basement room into an Art Deco treasure by using moldings and plywood. This handsome fireplace wall was created by combining 4×8 plywood sheets of rotary-sawn maple hardwood and solid poplar 1×3 battens—stained dark walnut—to cover the joints between sheets. The finish on the maple panels is water-base matte polyurethane to protect and enrich the look of the wood, without changing its color or adding glitzy sheen.

Material concerns

Moldings come in a variety of materials ranging from pine to hardwoods to high-density polyurethane. For simple painted molding designs, paint-grade wood is often the best choice.

When ornate detail is involved, however, molded polyurethane may be more economical. It is durable and lightweight, and won't split, rot, or warp. The downside is that polyurethane can't offer you the look of natural wood grain. It also may not be practical for baseboards or chair rails where the strength of wood better withstands the inevitable bumps and bashes.

Crowning touch

Crown molding defines a room and establishes its personality. Heavy, ornate designs can balance a high ceiling, while simpler profiles open up a smaller space. As a general rule, choose a maximum depth of ¾ inch for every vertical foot of wall; an 8-foot-high wall should wear a crown no more than 6 inches deep.

Best of all, when you combine treatments, the possibilities are limited only by the samples available; mix and match them to achieve a custom look for your home.

MOLDING INSTALLATION MADE EASY

Trim made with new manufacturing technology makes it easier than ever to achieve an elegant look. Ornate (and often heavy) moldings used to be painstakingly assembled from many carefully fitted pieces of wood, then painted and installed. The new high-tech moldings are made from lightweight urethane foam. Some even come with miterless corners, eliminating the need to cut precision mortars or cope cuts, and making installation that much easier.

Left: Eye-catching depth and popular Craftsman styling come to life with this creative use of standard plywood and lumber employed as moldings. Birch-veneer plywood panels are cleverly framed with a 5-foot-high chair rail and stiles effectively fashioned from 1×6 lumber.

Walls with Style

Right: **Wallpaper borders don't have to be restricted to the ceiling. Consider borders architectural elements on a roll. In this example, wallpapers and borders combine with paint to create a custom wall.**

Open your mind to the many techniques you can use to finish basement walls. Look beyond ordinary drywall to enhance the spaces.

When a room lacks architecture, create your own with a combination of wallpapers, borders, and paints. Below the chair rail, this space, *right,* gains a bold boost of color with striated wallpaper in a deep rose hue. Above the chair rail, a thin beribboned border frames the wall for charming detail. Walls inside the border are painted a soft sage green. To evoke a paneled look, a complementary floral border outlines a central rectangle of lighter cream; corner pieces add extra detail to this sophisticated and colorful wall treatment.

Plywood panels, spiced with gel stains, lend three-dimensional pizzazz to these plain basement walls. When it's time to redecorate, panels like these can be relocated in the room and may be restained or painted over.

Transform your basement in a weekend with coats of white paint to brighten concrete walls, and sheets of corrugated, galvanized steel to finish interior walls.

Wainscoting—created with plywood, 1x lumber, and moldings—extends to three-quarters height to give this room an elegant, traditional look. Whitening the woodwork provides pleasing contrast against other colors in the room and sets off furniture and accessories.

Floor Fashions

Right: Rather than covering these stair treads with standard carpeting, they're dressed in style by brushing floor-and-deck enamel over homemade stencils. Carefully follow the manufacturer's instructions on drying time between coats, and avoid high-gloss paints and finishes, which may be slippery.

Attractive basements begin with setting the stage and dressing up all the surfaces—including the floor. You'll discover a variety of materials—from paint and concrete to tiles and rugs—can help you achieve the look you want within budget. Put high fashion underfoot with these creative ideas.

CONCRETE CHARISMA

Although it looks like tile, this floor is concrete. The colored, mottled marblelike finish is created using an acid stain. To achieve the look, install a layer of rigid foam atop the existing slab of concrete to add insulation and to protect the decorative finish from cracks caused by shifting. Top the rigid foam with a 2-inch concrete cap stained with a base color and treated with a concrete hardener that will allow proper staining before finishing. After allowing the floor to cure for about 48 hours, score a pattern or border, or both, into the surface of the floor. Rub acid-base stains (pine and ebony hues were used here) into the patterned areas. The penetrating stain will chemically etch the surface with color and react with the hardening agent and base color to create this decorative effect. Varying shades and imperfections enhance the intended beauty of the form. Intensify color by increasing applications of stain. The color is permanent and won't fade or scuff. To finish the floor, fill the scored lines with grout and protect with acrylic sealer.

Left: An ordinary sisal rug is a stylish match with a wide painted-on border. To paint your own sisal rug, use latex paints, masking tape for crisp edges, and stencils for creating shapes and designs.

Below left: This one-of-a-kind tile border isn't as tricky as it appears. Simply cut a 2-inch square from one corner of each 6-inch tile, then "lap" the tiles in one direction. Be sure to leave a consistent 1/4-inch grout seam between tiles.

Below right: A zigzag strip of black vinyl cuts through a standard pattern of cream and blue vinyl tiles just as unexpectedly as a bolt of lightning.

Ceilings to Look Up To

Ceilings aren't going to be covered the way floors are covered with rugs and furniture. So why not invest in creative ceiling treatments for your basement rooms. Materials as simple as paint, wallcoverings, and moldings can make a dramatic difference in even the most ordinary room. Or consider experimenting with materials that are unusual in a basement, such as tin tiles or beaded board. Keep in mind, too, that suspended ceiling systems now come in more attractive designs and are still a practical choice if you want to have easy access to wiring and plumbing. Half the fun is finding or creating new ideas to try.

Right: Create a theme with a painted-on medallion. Here, a mariner's compass around the base of the pendant fixture echoes an old-world theme and creates easy and inexpensive architectural interest.

Right: The open ceiling in this rustic basement dining room is perfectly appropriate. Painting the joists and the spaces between them keeps the look light and clean.

BASEMENT BASICS

Painting a ceiling or decorating it with other materials, such as wood or wallcovering, can be tiring. Ask someone to help you with the project to make the work go faster. If you plan to paint exposed joists and all the works in between, consider renting a sprayer to complete the job sooner.

Left: Rough-sawn cedar planks complement this basement with a view of a woodland setting. Beaded ceiling board panels are another option for finishing the ceilings in your lower-level living spaces. Use molding to conceal seams.

Left and below: For this opulent powder room ceiling, thick embossed wallpaper was cut to fit. To achieve the effect of antique gilding on the ceiling, an undercoat of red paint was applied first and allowed to dry. Gold-metal leaf was brushed on and abraded with soft steel wool to reveal the texture of the embossed wall covering. The crown molding also was gilded and rubbed very lightly to reveal touches of red.

Window Dressings

Put your basement windows on the best-dressed list, and try these ideas to shake up the wardrobe. Fabric, for example, almost always fits the room when splashing a window with color and pattern. Tiny basement windows could use a short fabric valance or a fabric-covered wooden valance teamed with blinds for privacy, if needed. If there are no windows, then create one using lighting and shutters, such as the attractive faux window, *above.*

You can make the most of small windows, too, by helping them blend in with the setting instead of standing out. Rather than interrupt the lively painted backdrop in the basement playroom, *opposite bottom,* for example, the window continues the theme. The glass first was painted with paint

designed to create a frosted surface. The shapes were created with artist's oil paints that were hand-rubbed and blended for a translucent appearance. The stained-glass effect still allows light to flow in but provides privacy.

Left: Though this basement office sees sunlight coming in through one exterior window, the translucent panel admits a diffused warm glow created by natural and electric light in the adjoining room.

Below right: Jazz up a box-pleat valance with embellishments. Points of lace peek from the lower edge as daisy appliqués lend a colorful touch.

Below left: Rather than interrupt the lively painted backdrop in this basement playroom, the window continues the theme. The bright yellow and complementary tones help add brightness to the room.

Making Arrangements

Whether you want to show off photographs, prints, or paintings, there are lots of appealing ways to display artwork. You'll also be amazed at the creative and efficient ways you can arrange furniture, even in a small room. These simple guidelines will help you place artwork and furnishings like a design pro.

Artwork

■ Be careful not to hang artwork too high. Decide if you'll most often view the art while standing or sitting. Hang it at the corresponding eye level.

■ Unite a grouping and make it more impressive by using matching mats and frames; evenly space pictures close together to attract the eye.

■ Lay out a potential grouping on the floor first. One approach is to arrange pictures so the grouping's perimeter forms a geometric shape. One or two straight lines should run somewhere through the arrangement for the best look.

■ Make a small picture look more substantial with a wide mat and a large frame. For example, don't be afraid to put a 3½×5-inch print in an oversize mat and an 11×14-inch frame.

■ Do you like to change artwork often? Prop objects on easels, mantels, tables, shelves, or on the ubiquitous ledge found in the basement of new homes, such as in the lower-level family room, *opposite*.

■ Mats and frames don't have to match to make a grouping work. Common colors and subject matter can tie the arrangement nicely together.

Furniture

How you arrange the furnishings in your new basement spaces can influence comfort levels as well as appearance. Keep these tips in mind:

■ **Find the focal point.** The furniture grouping, *opposite,* centers on the coffee table, but you can focus the arrangement on any dominant point in the room. When designing a space, first find the focal point. An architectural feature—such as a fireplace, built-ins, or a window—is a natural focal point; in rooms without such structural features, create a center of interest with a large armoire, hutch, or bookcases.

■ **Avoid lining furniture along the walls.** Even in the small space, *opposite,* the furniture is arranged to promote a more comfortable conversation area. Here the sectional dominates while other seating pieces gather around and make the mix more visually complex. These pieces are only a few feet apart to promote easy, intimate conversation.

■ **Form a natural path.** When placing furniture, it's fine to direct traffic flow, but avoid forming an obvious "hall" through the space. For ease of movement, a traffic pattern can flow in front of the seating as well as

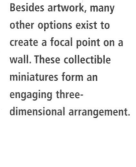

Besides artwork, many other options exist to create a focal point on a wall. These collectible miniatures form an engaging three-dimensional arrangement.

outside a grouping. Place chairs no more than 8 feet apart for conversation.

■ **Include tables and lighting.** Position a table within reach of every seating piece. Allow enough space to get through by placing the coffee table 14–18 inches from the sofa. Choose side tables that are about as tall as the arm of the chair or sofa. If possible, place a lamp near each seating area. Place lighting diagonally across the room if you have two lamps. If you have three, create a triangle to ensure aesthetic balance and an evenly lit space.

An L-shape sectional sofa makes the most of a small family room with cozy yet spacious seating. Reading materials and beverages are within easy reach of the coffee table.

Built-In Beauty

Douglas fir cabinetry frames this media center that has a retractable theater screen, speakers, and storage for equipment. Be sure to include pullouts for compact discs and DVDs, such as the slide-out compartment, *right*.

Built-in storage and seating help make the most of your basement living space while giving it a custom look. This basement features handsome Douglas fir cabinetry that instills warmth as well as an abundance of display and specialized entertainment options. Black accents give the built-ins an air of sophistication and elegance, while silvery metal pulls and bars inject contemporary style.

BASEMENT BASICS

The cabinetry shown here was custom built, but you can achieve a similar look using stock cabinetry augmented with features and embellishments. Remove cabinet doors, for example, paint the interior of the cabinet, and add lighting to create open display shelves or a display niche. Add moldings and divided inserts for unique style and to store specific items, such as DVDs and wine bottles.

Above: Space between studs can be carved out to form niches for artwork, such as this one. Add a spotlight to emphasize the display as a focal point. Left: Including a built-in wet bar requires only a small alcove. Set into a niche next to the wall of cubbyholes, this wet bar repeats the use of Douglas fir cabinetry. A granite countertop and stainless-steel shelf supports pack a lot of style into minimal space.

Right: A sump pump doesn't have to be a basement eyesore. This attractive entertainment and storage unit also hides a sump pump in one lower cabinet on the left. A lower cabinet on the right conceals the plumbing clean-out.

Below: Built-in seating in this lower-level family room doubles as storage with drawers hidden below the cushions.

In this media area, a handsome maple cabinet disguises a big-screen television. To minimize the cabinet size, it's flanked with stepped-back maple built-ins and weighty steel columns. Wafer-thin steel shelves slide into grooves in the wall units.

METAL URGES

Steel support columns are a common basement element. Boxing in columns with drywall and adding moldings is an attractive alternative, but this basement remodeling transforms the posts into decorative features. In this case, the unfinished columns were treated with a mild acid solution (similar to "gun blue" used to treat metal on guns), which oxidizes on the surface, blackens the steel, and makes the color integral to the metal surface.

A bed tucked away in the basement can serve as guest quarters or a comfortably cool napping spot. This bunk is a boxed-in twin mattress mounted to the wall on top of side-by-side chests. The interior is fitted with a wall-mounted reading lamp and a skinny wall shelf along the bed to hold a radio, books, and a glass of water. Thick curtains hang from a closet rod and can be drawn closed for privacy.

Peg
Your
Plan

Your dreams are taking shape—the basement is prepared, and you have a vision. Here's what you need to know to get your project rolling.

Opposite: Design and building professionals can make your basement rooms better than you imagined. If you're considering a media room, such as one like this, consider hiring an electronics contractor to get the most for your investment. Find out more about working with these pros on page 124–125.

Now that you have your plan—but before putting it to work—you need to review it. That's why you'll appreciate the start-to-finish overview that follows; refer to it often as your plans progress. After you've drafted the floor plan, move on to estimating the costs and deciding who will do the work. If you plan to hire a contractor, use the advice in this chapter to obtain bids, sort through the estimates, and make the best choices. Consider, too, having your ideas reviewed by design professionals, such as an architect, a design/build team, or an interior designer. Take a look at the services these pros offer and discover the ways each could refine and improve your basement rooms. With all the wonderful possibilities available for remodeling your basement, it's easy to go over budget. Keep the list of budget-saving basics on your nightstand or refrigerator door and use them as reminders to guide decisions that affect the budget. Finally, take the necessary steps to limit disruptions that remodeling can cause. All of your preliminary work is your ticket to discovering how much you can enjoy the remodeling journey that will take you to the finished basement of your dreams.

Start to Finish

The task of remodeling your basement might feel overwhelming, but the undertaking is much less so when it's broken down into smaller steps. Take a look at this progression of work, then keep the list handy as a reassuring guide and as a measure of your progress.

■ **Collect ideas.** Get a sense of what others have done with their basements. You already started this phase in Chapter 1 of this book, but don't stop there. Flip through magazines, books, and brochures for more. Put some three-ring pocket folders in a three-ring binder. When you see an idea you like, clip it and drop it into one of the folders. Mark clippings so you remember what you liked about them—maybe a layout, surface material, or decorative technique. As thoughts come to you, jot down notes about how you want to finish the space and your ideas for using it. Assign a pocket to those notes as well. You'll feel more confident knowing that you don't have to remember these ideas because the binder will remind you. Devote at least a month to this phase—some people spend a year or two. If you do spend that much time, you get a good sense of what you like and will be prepared to act when your needs for more living space begin to demand action.

■ **Gather facts** about your available space and your needs. Local real estate appraisers can help you get a feel for improvements that are appropriate for your neighborhood. The time to get a real feel for your basement transformation potential is before your need for space begins to cramp your living style. "Crack the Codes" on page 36 can help you learn about visiting your city's building department to discuss space and needs in broad terms, and find out what's possible and what's not. You'll also determine whether your space is weathertight and if not, how to take the steps to make it so. See "Eliminate Moisture" beginning on page 28 for more details. Many homeowners weatherproof their unfinished basements and test them through a few seasons to be confident they're ready to remodel when the time comes. There's no time like the present to

work through the section "Bids, Estimates, and Money" on page 122; it helps bring your needs and wants into focus.

■ **Start your idea machine.** You know your space; you know your needs. Put them together and start shaping possibilities by sketching initial floor plans. Get a sense of how you might draw light into the basement and fit in a full bathroom. Chapters 3 and 4 are your primary plan-development resources. At this phase of the job, you might call on an architect or designer for help (see page 124), as their experienced eyes often see solutions you may overlook. If you seek outside design help, you still can do as much of the work as you like. Plan to spend several weeks to several months in the idea-crafting stage. You'll live with the results for many years, so it's a good investment.

■ **Check out materials.** Shopping for materials before you fine-tune your plans may seem premature, but what you choose—in terms of both construction and surface materials—has an impact on your final direction. So collect those ideas and drop them into your binder. You may have been looking at materials from the moment you decided to remodel, or maybe not. Spend some time thinking about what you plan to use before you move on to the next stage.

■ **Move your plans toward detail.** Rough plans need to become firm in order to implement them. You need to figure every detail—from storage and utilities to finishing methods and decorative trims. If you go this far designing the basement spaces on your own, consider engaging an architect or a building designer to review your plans. They can spare you the trouble and expense of oversights later. Give yourself a couple of months in this phase. Chapter 4 helps you move from the planning stage to the implementation stage.

■ **Hone your choices.** This step can be difficult, but eliminating details or amenities that won't fit your budget or time frame has to be done. Gathering ideas can be easy, but separating them into wants versus must-haves is more difficult. Don't despair! Hang on to that great wet bar idea, for example, that you can't work into the budget today. Perhaps you can run the plumbing lines now and install the cabinets, sink and faucet, countertop, and wine chiller in the future.

■ **Decide who will do the work.** Perhaps you want to do the remodeling work yourself, or maybe you've always planned to hire it out. Now is the time to give the topic serious consideration; track down your general contractor or subcontractors, and prepare your space for transformation. The section "Who Will Do the Work" on page 122 walks you through these decisions. Allow two months for this stage.

■ **Prepare for the actual work.** If you're doing the work yourself, it's time to apply for building permits and prepare a calendar of work, material-ordering dates, and inspections that will take place along the way. Building permits are good for only a limited amount of time; discuss scheduling—plus inspections—with your city's building department. It's also time to prepare the rest of your home for the remodeling effort: Relocate activities, reroute entries, protect traffic routes through the house, and arrange for dumpsters, if necessary. A couple of weeks, if that, is all you need for this effort.

■ **Order materials.** You'll need to order materials several times throughout the project, arranging for them to arrive when you need them. If you have ample storage space available, such as in the garage, you can order items even further ahead. Keep in mind, however, that plans could change (such as an unforeseen structural obstacle) that would make the item unusable and often unreturnable.

■ **Strap on a tool belt** and start your project. The transformation project is now under way! The first order of business is to take care of demolition and tackle major structural and mechanical work. Build stairs, move mechanical elements, reroute utility lines, rough in ductwork and under-floor drains, and replace old plumbing fixtures.

■ **Frame your rooms.** Now is the time to frame rooms and install windows and exterior and interior doors. This phase completes the skeleton of your finished basement. The

length of time this and any of the following steps require varies with the scope and complexity of the project, the time you have available to work, and whether you're working alone or with a helper. If you hire out the work, the process moves more quickly.

■ **Install internal systems.** After the walls are framed, run wires, pipes, and ducts for water, gas, electric, and climate control. Install nail plates on framing pieces to prevent nails from being driven through utility lines. Take pictures of the lines in place now in case you forget to mark them on the covering drywall. Finally insulate the walls— including the ceilings and interior walls that you want to soundproof.

■ **Add finishing touches.** Your project is in the homestretch! Install wall and ceiling surfaces—often drywall, but occasionally paneling or a suspended ceiling. Then it's time to paint and install trim and flooring.

■ **Your basement living spaces are complete!** Commemorate your hard work with a gathering and a toast. Have someone take your photographs in the new space. Tuck photographs of the project's progression into an album, or use your planning binder as an album to share your efforts and hard work with friends and family.

Bids, Estimates, and Money

People are naturally leery of adding up the costs, but budgeting doesn't have to be stressful if you follow these guidelines and bag the best bid, land a good loan, and avoid contractual headaches.

Obtaining bids

The bidding process is the same whether you're gathering a bid on a complete project from a general contractor or on a portion of the work from a subcontractor. Request bids based on your plans from a handful of the contractors you meet initially. If you want to include specific appliances or features in your project, list them and give the list to the bidding contractors. Three weeks is a reasonable amount of time for each of them to get back to you with a bid. When bids return, expect specific, itemized materials lists; a schedule noting what will be done when and when payments will be made based on that progress; and the contractor's fee. Bid prices are not necessarily predictors of the quality of work or materials to be used, so ask contractors to explain their bids in detail.

Preparing your own estimate

If you'll be doing most of the work, determine costs by breaking work into manageable chunks, starting with costs for waterproofing or insulating; then framing, plumbing, electrical, and construction; then finish work. Rather than shopping at many different stores for the best prices on individual items, find one home center and lumber source that offers reasonable prices and top-notch service. Save time and hassle by getting to know the staff at the store you choose. Visit when the store isn't busy, and share your plans with the staff. A good salesperson can become a valuable adviser when you're estimating what each phase of your project will cost.

Be ready for the 10-15 rule

No matter how carefully you or your contractors prepare bids, savvy homeowners know that a remodeling project usually ends up costing 10 to 15 percent more than estimated. Unexpected complexities and changes are commonplace. After hammers start swinging, enthusiastic homeowners often upgrade plans and materials, figuring that "as long as we've gone to this much trouble, let's go further." Spare yourself hassle and headache by anticipating budget overruns.

Contracts

Bids are in; you've chosen your contractors. The next step is to protect everyone involved with a written contract that includes:

■ A detailed description of work to be done by the contractor and subcontractors, and work to be done by you. Include demolition and construction responsibilities.

■ A schedule of work that also describes how delays will be handled and when payments will be made.

■ A description of materials used.

■ Protective elements that include a right-of-recision clause that gives you a short period of time to back out of the project; proof of bonding and an insurance certificate; and a warranty that guarantees work and materials for at least one year. Finally, a mechanic's lien waiver protects you from having a lien placed against your property if your contractor doesn't pay the subcontractors.

■ Statements that specify who secures building permits and arranges inspections.

■ A statement about change orders and how modifications or last-minute additions to the work will be handled.

■ A statement that guarantees final walk-through and approval preceding final payment. During that walk-through, point out anything that is not to your satisfaction. Allow the contractor a reasonable amount of time to remedy unsatisfactory situations.

Who will do the work?

You have four options—each has advantages and disadvantages—for getting work done.
■ **Do all or most of the work yourself.** If you have the tools, skills, time, inclination, energy, and physical ability, you can save a

lot of money by doing much of the work yourself; but before you tear into a big project, do a self-assessment. Total up the cost of the additional tools, if any, you'll have to buy or rent to get the project done. Account for the time it will take you to order and pick up materials and learn techniques. If you plan to take time off from work to complete the project, compute the cost of lost earnings. Then consider the cost of a potential mistake in both time and money. Miscutting a piece of drywall may cost a few dollars in wasted material and a few minutes of time (if you've purchased an extra sheet or two for just such a situation). Miscutting a piece of sheet vinyl flooring or expensive carpet might cost a lot more. Wrestling with heavy materials or trying to work long hours to maintain a schedule sometimes results in injury, an even greater cost. It actually may be cheaper and less risky to hire out some jobs, such as laying carpet or sheet flooring, or extensive wiring or plumbing modifications. Hiring out allows you to concentrate on jobs that better suit your skills, physical condition, confidence level, and available tools.

■ **Do some of the work yourself** and hire out the rest. One way is to act as general contractor; another is to hire a general contractor. Either way, you pencil yourself in as the responsible party for certain tasks. Be sure to stick to schedule. Here are some strategies for sorting out who does what:

Manage the materials. Order, purchase, and arrange delivery of supplies yourself.

Be a laborer. Do work that requires more labor than materials and skill, such as demolition, excavating, insulating, and painting.

Do the costly work. If you have the skills and tools, and if code allows, tackle the plumbing or electrical tasks, and leave less specialized efforts to others.

Be an apprentice. Ask your contractor to leave minor jobs—such as daily cleanup—for you to do.

■ **Hire a general contractor.** You may also decide to hire a general contractor to complete the entire project. This is the most comprehensive approach to getting your renovation completed. You hire one person with broad construction expertise to manage materials, inspections, and supervise the work of many others. That person is your primary contact.

Find a licensed contractor by asking friends and colleagues to recommend contractors who have successfully completed jobs in their homes. Get several names and meet with each. Seeking out a contractor is time-consuming, but it's critical; the right contractor could become your partner for a succession of projects. When you meet with each contractor, discuss plans, ask about experience with similar projects, and how the contractor would approach this one. Ask how much the project might cost—not as a formal, contractual estimate but to get an idea of the contractor's familiarity with the work. Before the meeting ends, ask for proof of bonding (to ensure work will be completed), proof of insurance that covers on-the-job injuries, and—most important—references. Talk to at least two customers who have had projects done that are similar to yours. Ask whether the work was done on time, on budget, and to their satisfaction. Arrange to see the work so you can assess quality firsthand. Also ask to view a couple of ongoing projects and talk to those homeowners.

■ **Be your own general contractor.** If your skills are more administrative than technical, filling the role of general contractor can be a source of pride. Be aware that this job is also extremely time-consuming and challenging. As a general contractor, you manage the purchase and delivery of materials, hire subcontractors, communicate plans to each, coordinate work schedules and inspections, and pay everyone. Select subcontractors carefully. Most subcontractors favor professional contractors over armchair generals because professionals are more likely to be a steady source of income. Before making the decision to be your own general contractor, talk to other people with skills or time constraints similar to your own and find out what lessons and advice they have to offer. Also check local book stores and the Internet for the numerous guides and checklists available for anyone preparing to tackle the task.

Budget Basics

Eventually your basement remodeling blueprints translate into to green dollars. Try these tips to bring your project to the finish line on budget.

Staying on budget with your basement remodeling begins with clearly explaining your budget to your architect or contractor from the beginning. It continues with picking a reputable contractor who doesn't low-ball the estimate or complete the project you with substandard work. Just as important, it takes informed decisionmaking at all steps—from price estimates through the little changes you make along the way. Here are some ways to reap savings:

■ Can you simplify the design? Take another look at premium architectural features, such as curved walls or fancy ceiling treatments. Separate frills from essentials.

■ Can you substitute less-expensive materials? Today great looks come in a wide price range. You may be able to splurge in a few crucial spots by economizing elsewhere.

■ Can you remodel in phases? Consider deferring built-ins, for example, that are secondary to the main project. Plan accordingly. Pre-wire for home office equipment and the media room, for example. Then add built-ins and electronic equipment later.

■ Can you do some of the work yourself? Demolition, painting, tiling, and cleanup are popular do-it-yourself jobs. You and your contractor should agree on the value of the work from the outset, and don't take on a job unless you can do it correctly and on schedule.

Be wary of budget busters that can sneak up during the best-planned project. Some costs, such as fixing hidden damage, are difficult to foresee until the contractor makes the discovery. But it's reasonable to expect a conscientious contractor to anticipate common budget busters, such as building code requirements. Your best protection against unpleasant surprises is to anticipate trouble at the outset. Chat with neighbors who have remodeled the basements of similar homes. Call your building department and become thoroughly familiar with the applicable building codes. Point out potential problem areas to your contractor. Always ask if there's anything that could increase costs down the road.

After work begins, cost control can become your own worst enemy. As the basement remodeling shapes up, you'll inevitably see additional work you'd like done or features you'd like added. Resist the temptation to upgrade "while we're at it." After you have a plan and budget, resolve to stay within the scope of the work. If you don't, it's hard to stop. If you find you've made a mistake that you simply won't allow, discuss it with your contractor immediately. Relocating a new wall is a lot less costly at the framing stage, for example, than after that same wall has wiring or plumbing added. Every change from the original plan should be documented by a written change order that you or your contractor sign, describing the change and stating the costs. That way there won't be any unpleasant debate at the end of the project about who said what. After all, the best surprise in a remodeling project is a final bill that's exactly what you expected.

Survive the remodeling

Good news: Basement remodeling is low-stress work. The out-of-the-way location of the basement means that you can close the door on the mess.

Opposite: If your budget is tight, you always can depend on paint to enliven a plain concrete floor or ordinary drywall. Create this back-to-nature look that's better than expensive wallpaper. Trace leaf shapes onto stencil acetate. Cut out the shapes with a crafts knife and apply stencils randomly to the wall using a stencil roller. Use a slightly damp rag to dab and smudge the stenciled images before they dry.

BIDDING WARS

Nothing is more confusing than sending a remodeling plan out for bids and getting back wildly different estimates. When bids are all over the map, take some time to find out why:

Review the bids and specs with each contractor to make sure you have an apples-to-apples comparison on materials and design assumptions.

Ask about how the work will be accomplished. You may find that one contractor is more resourceful than another at finding solutions for construction problems. But don't just settle for the low bid. You may discover that a low bidder hasn't anticipated important problems.

Question each contractor to learn whether any bid might have neglected significant costs. Costs that contractors often overlook or underestimate include demolition, permit fees, disposal of debris, and repair to landscaping. Ask if the bid includes the price of bringing old systems up to code where required.

Review your notes from your reference checks on each contractor. Avoid a contractor who consistently finds lots of expensive surprises during construction.

Still you can ease the process for you and your family if you do some planning:

■ Remove activity areas from the space during remodeling. It's tough to do laundry, for example, in a room full of sawdust.

■ Close off entries. If your family usually goes in and out of the space you're remodeling, have them use other entries. Hang several sheets of plastic, floor to ceiling, around doors that separate the work area from the rest of your home. Also seal off vents in the work area with plastic to prevent dust and grime from getting into the ductwork and filtering throughout the house.

■ Identify the path you want contractors (or anyone else) to use to move through the house. Protect floors along this path by taping heavy plastic sheeting over them.

■ Sweep and clean up daily. Dust, grime, and scraps that travel into the house on your shoes are tough on floors and carpet.

■ Schedule a time each day to discuss project progress and situations. This may well be the most important tip, whether you're doing the work or hiring it out. Reviewing

WHEN TO DO-IT-YOURSELF

Even homeowners with generous budgets sometimes like to roll up their sleeves to get the job done. Trouble is, most of us don't have time to do all of the hands-on work, and some tasks require tools and skills that are anything but ordinary.

When sweat equity makes sense, by all means dig in, but leave more complicated jobs to experienced tradespeople. A do-it-yourselfer might do light demolition, painting, installing moldings, ceramic tile work, installing a faucet, and wallpapering. Here are three other tasks many amateurs can tackle:

Simple framing. Home improvement guidebooks can help, so simple jobs, such as framing a partition wall, lie within reach of do-it-yourselfers. Complications may include existing electrical or plumbing systems; no one should try these or larger structural framing without training.

Drywall. Hanging and taping drywall is a relatively simple task—if you can measure accurately—though it is time-consuming and a little tedious. The material can be fastened with special cup-head nails. Driving drywall screws with a portable or cordless drill yields better long-term results and allows you to shift or remove and reinstall panels (before taping) without damaging them.

Cabinet installation. Although it takes a serious investment in equipment and training to build cabinets, installing stock cabinetry requires fewer tools and skills. Most manufacturers anticipate the likelihood of DIY remodeling and package installation instructions with the cabinets.

the day's progress after coming home tired and hungry could be stressful and lead to rash judgments. Try to hold off reviews until everyone has had dinner and a chance to relax.

Consider the Pros

An architect dreamed up the welcoming Southwestern flair for this lower-level family room. Loaded with the kinds of ideas that a professional might bring to your own remodeling plans, this inspired space features an adobe-style fireplace distinguished by stepped display shelves and storage niches that are both practical and good-looking. The built-in seating helps define the room while making the setting cozy and inviting. If you don't plan to work with an architect on your project, consider using an interior designer teamed with a carpenter for some creative results.

Three types of design professionals are available to help with your basement project. Although they have specialized areas of expertise, most professionals are well-versed in all phases of design and can help create a comprehensive plan.

ARCHITECTS are familiar with many types of building materials, finishes, and appliances, and have thorough knowledge of structural, electrical, plumbing, heating, ventilation, and air-conditioning systems. Plans that include structural changes to your house and must be reviewed by your local building and planning commission should be prepared by an architect or structural engineer. Architects charge a percentage of the total cost of the project, usually 10 to 15 percent; or you can hire an architect on an hourly basis. For a listing of architects in your area, visit the website of the American Institute of Architects at www.aia.org.

INTERIOR DESIGNERS work with colors, wall finish treatments, fabrics, floor coverings, furnishings, lighting, and accessories to personalize a shape and create a cohesive look. Interior designers are familiar with building codes and structural requirements. They can also make recommendations for placement of partition walls, plumbing hookups, electrical outlets, and architectural details. However, project plans may need to be approved by the local building and planning commission, and structural changes may require a structural engineer or registered architect. Interior designers certified by the American Society of Interior Designers (ASID) must demonstrate an ongoing knowledge of materials, building codes, government regulations, and safety standards. For more information, visit the ASID website at www.asid.org.

DESIGN/BUILD TEAMS offer complete project management from initial design to completion of construction. To do their job they become thoroughly familiar with the building methods and techniques specified by the project plan. Design/build teams may not offer the services of an architect so plan for an architect or structural engineer to approve structural modifications. Design/build teams generally don't offer interior design services.

Hiring a design pro can yield delightful details by the dozens, such as those in this family room. They include a shapely fireplace with handmade tile surround, handsome built-in bookcases with a custom spot for the big-screen television, and a sophisticated lighting cove near the ceiling.

Contributors/Resources

Pages 4–7
Field Editor: Cathy Kramer
Field Scout: Bill Nolan, Lithe Lines
Photographer: Geoff Johnson, Malone & Company Photography
Architect: CK designs, Cramer Kreski Designs, (412) 895-3165
Interior Designer: Doris Buell, ASID, (412) 493-3165
Contractor: Tackett Co., Residential and commercial builders, (412) 895-1979
Furnishings: Ethan Allen, Kelly Maicon, representative (203) 743-8000 ext. 8575
Plant stand #45-9011; chair side chest #24-5406/620 finish; coffee table #24-8401/620 finish; end table/nightstand #24-5416/620 finish
Rugs: The Rug Market, (323) 930-0202, Style # 23076, Canon, in natural/black
Lamps: Artemide, Marcy Iken, representative, (631) 694-9292, Style #009048, Tizio classic lamp, black
Pillows: Pier 1

Pages 26–27, 61, 68, 96
Barrington Junior Women's Club Designer Showhouse, Barrington, IL
Field Editor: Elaine Markoutsas
Photographer: Guy Hurka
Design: Pat Bailey, ASID with Anne Cullinane, Donna Hall, Susan Klimala, Mary K. Plass
Interior Design Department
College of DuPage
425 Fawell Boulevard
Glen Ellyn, IL 60137
(630) 942-2800 ext. 5210
Ragging and metallic finish: Interior Illusions, Inc., Kelly Whitt, Page Tantillo, (815) 439-5900
Paint: ICI, Dulux Paint Centers, (800) 984-5444
Furniture, rugs, lamps, artwork: Toms-Price, (630) 668-7878 ext. 1113

Fabrics:
Fabricut, (800) 999-8200, Plum ultrasuede: #13597-12, Basil: #13597/10
Design Tex Fabric, (312) 321-1204, Canterbury: 1019-301, Chalice
Robert Allen, (800) 240-8189, Diamond: Razzamataz-cinnabar, Dot: Dewdrop-henna, Stripe: Naropa-Aubergine
Window Treatments:
Fabric, Unika Vaev Fabric, (800) 237-1625, Look Twice-Brick 47151
Fabrication, Mimsie O'Hara Fabric Designs, (630) 789-3043
Accessories (including candles, prints, glassware, sconces, rods): The Great Indoors, (847) 874-8006

Page 39
Decorative window well liner:
Scenic Window Wells
1211 Barclay Circle
Inverness, IL 60010
(866) 935-5723
www.wellliner.com

Page 45
Air-gap/drainage membrane:
Cosella-Dorken
Delta-Fl
(888) 433-5824
www.deltams.com

Page 50
Quiet Zone soundproofing materials:
Owens Corning
(800) 438-7465
www.owenscorning.com

Index